KEVIN
MALONE

with Stephen Copeland

MW00424165

SCOUTING
THE ENEMY

From Running Major League Baseball Teams
to Ending Child Sex Trafficking

PROCEEDS OF THIS BOOK WILL GO TO FIGHT CHILD SEX TRAFFICKING.

Scouting the Enemy
From Running Major League Baseball Teams to Ending Child Sex Trafficking

by Kevin Malone
with Stephen Copeland

www.malone-scoutingtheenemy.com

Copyright © 2023 by Kevin Malone

Published by The Core Media Group, Inc., www.thecoremediagroup.com.
Cover & Interior Design: Nadia Guy

ISBN 978-1-950465-92-7

All rights reserved. No part of this publication may be reproduced, stored in a retrieval system, or transmitted in any form or by any means—electronic, mechanical, photocopy, recording, scanning, or other—except for brief quotation in printed reviews, without the prior written permission of the publisher.

Unless otherwise noted, Scripture quotations are taken from The Holy Bible, New International Version®, NIV®, Copyright © 1973, 1978, 1984, 2011 by Biblica, Inc.® Used by permission. All rights reserved worldwide.

Printed in the United States of America.

CONTENTS

INTRODUCTION

I had it all.

Waking up one day and realizing that you are overseeing one of the most iconic organizations in all of American sports, the Los Angeles Dodgers, is a bizarre experience. I had access to Hollywood's stars and always had free tickets to special events like concerts and Lakers games. Wherever I wanted to go, whatever I wanted to do, I could usually do it. It is even more bizarre to realize that you don't like the view from the top.

My identity had long been tied up in baseball. I am very blessed to have had the professional journey I had in baseball, as my quick rise as a scout eventually led to serving as an assistant general manager on one Major League Baseball team, the Baltimore Orioles, and as a General Manager for two different MLB organizations, the Montreal Expos and the Dodgers. That journey ended bizarrely in 2001, when a media firestorm led to my resignation. More about that later.

At the time, I thought being out of baseball was the worst thing that could happen to me. I had been leading a big-market team on the largest stage, and the public humiliation was almost too much to bear. But it turned out to be the best thing that ever happened to me. That's right, the *best* thing that ever happened to me. That experience was the beginning of my path to ministry and activism, toward *truly* helping and serving others. I had to evaluate my self-worth and what I should do next.

I thought a lot about one of my favorite Old Testament heroes, Moses. Other than Jesus, I suppose Moses is the Biblical character who I look up to the most. My prayer is that my journey—in some small way—reflects Moses's route toward purpose and a liberation-centered mission that is clearly led by God. The Exodus is one of the most well-known stories in the Old Testament, and I believe Moses's journey can provide something of a blueprint for each of us—one that leads to purpose and, ultimately, justice. Moses would learn that these two things went hand-in-hand, which I believe is a universal call to each of us.

We are each called to a purpose. We are each called to make this world a better place. I like to think of this as redemptive justice. We are called to be taken into the loving arms of God. We are called to lead lives that are bigger than ourselves. As Mark Twain once wrote, "The two most important days in your life are the day you are born and the day you find out why."

So, what is your *why?* Consider Matthew 5:16—"Let your light so shine before men, that they may see your good works, and glorify your Father which is in heaven." Another verse I love is Ephesians 2:10—"For we are God's handiwork, created in Christ Jesus to do good works, which God prepared in advance for us to do." Our why brings hope and points people toward the Father.

The chapters ahead will jump around from story to story regarding the unique life I've been blessed to live. Some of the stories are heavy. Other stories are entertaining, especially for sports fans. Many of my stories are flat-out bizarre. The *Los Angeles Times* once described me as a "fascinating, ever-changing, complex guy." But please know that this book is not about me—it is not an autobiography. It has elements of a memoir, but the sole purpose of talking about the varying aspects of my life is to hopefully connect with you and empower *you* in your own life. You might disagree with some of my faith-based convictions. That's okay. I hope each chapter at least gets you thinking.

Whether you're an activist, minister, leader of a nonprofit, volunteer, or someone who has been on the sidelines far too long, I hope this collection of stories will move your soul to action and help you construct a championship team around your cause. I hope they encourage you to refine your thinking as much as it spurs you into action. I hope these stories help give you the confidence to take everything you have experienced—even your deepest pains—and use them for the good of others.

This book invites you to find your own purpose, one that is related to justice and making this world a better place. As a seeker of God, I believe justice is integral to our purpose as humans. We are each called, in our own ways, to serve the "least of these" (Matthew 25:40), to love others in both our "actions and in truth" (1 John 3:18), to "defend the weak and the fatherless" and "uphold the cause of the poor and the oppressed" (Psalm 82:3-4). Faith without action is dead—it has no value.

Each person should care about justice. Every human needs to be treated with dignity and fairness. I like the term "restorative justice," which I interpret to mean seeking out vulnerable people who are being taken advantage of or exploited and helping them. We are to open our mouths for those who can't speak for themselves, to be a voice for the voiceless. We are to help rescue the disadvantaged, to make other people's problems *our* problems.

You don't have to be a Christian to read this book, though I believe learning about *elohei mishpat*, the Hebrew name for the God of justice who calls us into service, can help us expand our imaginations to find our true purpose in life. I believe learning about Jesus of Nazareth—whose life and ministry were centered on serving others, especially those on the margins of society who were neglected or abused—can anchor us in difference-making values as we pursue our unique purpose. I hope by opening up to you about my own life and mistakes that you will trust more deeply a God who is guiding you in your transformation.

Are you ready to live a more purposeful life and help bring healing to the world?

PART I
PURPOSE

1
LOST BUT FOUND

"But when she could hide him no longer, she got a papyrus basket for him and coated it with tar and pitch. Then she placed the child in it and put it among the reeds along the bank of the Nile."
~Exodus 2:3

I woke up the morning of July 2, 2013, and heard horrific sounds coming from my son's bedroom, something that sounded like a mixture between a cough and a choke. I rushed to his room.

It had not been a good weekend in the Malone household. Our son, Shawn, twenty-three years old, was back from a semester abroad at the University of Melbourne in Australia through the University of Southern California. Since returning to the States, he had jumped back into a lifestyle of bingeing and partying.

Shawn drank and smoked pot in high school, but his drug use escalated in college at USC, as he began experimenting with hard drugs like Roxy and cocaine. Before he had gone to Australia, I had gotten into a fight with him. Knowing he had drugs in his system, I tried to stop him from getting behind the wheel of a car. Shawn, who wrecked four cars in high school and college, took the keys and shoved me to the ground. That was our only physical altercation, and my heart was broken. Our son was lost.

My wife, Marilyn, and I suspected that if he continued to living the way he was, we'd one day get a call that he had killed himself or somebody else. What were we to do? He was an adult. We had tried everything to get his attention. We felt like we had done everything we could to raise him in a Christian household, let him know he was loved and accepted, and lay a spiritual foundation for him.

What had we done wrong?

His semester abroad in Australia seemed to help detach him from the culture of darkness he found at USC. When I picked up Shawn from the airport, he showed me a tattoo, written in Hebrew, that he had gotten on his chest. It said "Elohim," the name used for God in Hebrew Scriptures.

No skulls or crossbones? I thought to myself. *What was going on with my son?*

Seeing how God seemed to be working on him in Australia made me choke up and hide my tears on the way home. But that was short-lived.

A weekend binge with his old friends reignited past behaviors, and Shawn began using drugs again. Marilyn and I felt this could lead to him spiraling down into addiction.

I stood by his bedroom door that morning, wondering if the noise I heard was some kind of groggy snore. That's when I heard the same choking sound once again. I burst into the room and saw him unconscious, severely struggling to breathe.

He had overdosed.

I screamed for Marilyn as our son's life flashed before our eyes. He was rushed to Providence Saint John's Health Center in Santa Monica, where we learned that Shawn had not only done drugs the night before with his friends but had likely done more in his room when he got home early that morning, as fresh drugs were in his system. In addiction, one's appetite is never quite fulfilled.

His brain had suffered a series of strokes and was now nonfunctional. Doctors told us his body was shutting down—that he was dying! While at the hospital, I contacted everyone I could, asking for prayers and begging for a miracle. Shawn entered a coma, and helplessness fell upon us.

As the days passed, my wife, my daughter Shannon, and my "adopted" son from Uganda, Peter, tried to cling to hope, but we found ourselves slowly confronting what seemed to be the inevitable. The neurologist kept saying that if he ever woke up from his coma, he would remain in a vegetative state the rest of his life. We were told that the time was approaching for us to consider removing his feeding tube and starving him to death.

Final Sign of Hope

Four or five days into Shawn's coma, I was in Shawn's hospital room with one of my good friends, Tracy Williams. Tracy and I were talking to Shawn and praying for him. When we opened our eyes after our heartfelt crying out to God, we noticed a single tear emerge from Shawn's eye. It began to stream down his face slowly.

When we told the doctors and nurses about what had happened, they said it was nothing more than a strange coincidence—that the body can do bizarre things during a coma. After all, his brain showed severely limited activity. But Tracy and I knew what we had seen. For almost a week, Shawn had been entirely unresponsive. What were the chances he'd shed a tear *while* we were praying?

During the first few days, Shannon's fighting spirit (like her dad) showed up in a big way. Whereas Marilyn and I remained in a stupor from the shock of it all, Shannon reminded us of the stakes we faced and the need to act *now*. She would say, "Dad, we *have* to do something. The doctors are saying they can't help Shawn. We have to find a hospital that can help him."

A week or so into his coma, I had Shannon and her now-husband Carlos bring a little container that was once filled with marijuana to the hospital. Welcome to California. We hovered the container beneath Shawn's nose, and, I kid you not, a slight grin appeared on Shawn's face. It was as if he knew we were messing with him, trying anything we could to get a reaction out of him.

But that was the last sign of hope. We again entered a lengthy phase of deep unknowing. The hospital bills piled up. Shawn was moved to the UCLA hospital for the next two weeks and showed no signs of improvement. A month into his coma, we were again told that the inevitable was upon us. Even if he did awaken, he'd likely have no semblance of a normal life.

One evening, my friend Francis Chan and his daughter joined my family in Shawn's hospital room as we knelt beside Shawn's bed and desperately cried out to God. By the end of Francis' prayer, we saw several large tears streaming down Shawn's face. It was as if Shawn was trying to communicate with us. It was as if he was letting us know that, though brain scans showed his mind to be entirely nonfunctional, he was with us in some way. With his heart. With his soul.

He was reaching out to us through the void.

We decided to have Shawn air-ambulanced to Craig Hospital in Englewood, Colorado, a hospital specializing in spinal cord injuries and traumatic brain injuries. We were hopeful they would be able to give us some answers. They monitored him closely, but Shawn showed no responsiveness. No more smiles when we hovered the marijuana container beneath his nose. No more tears during desperate prayers. Had Shawn broken down during Francis's prayer because he was, in some way, telling us goodbye? Was this his final interaction with us?

I kept trying to trust that somehow, some way, he was with us in body, soul, and spirit. I intentionally put earbuds in his ears during his coma so he would hear sermons, worship songs, and Scripture. We talked to him like he was still with us.

But then reality began to settle in again. Before we knew it, fifty days had passed. The doctors and nurses at Craig Hospital gave us what felt like *slightly* more positive encouragement. Still, they were probably just providing us with more information since they were on the frontlines of research around traumatic brain injuries. Down the hall, all the rooms were full of Traumatic Brain Injury patients. The atmosphere there was challenging—so many young and older people in various stages of TBI. Hope was non-existent. Walking through the hospital hallways felt like we were walking through a cloud of palpable despair.

Lazarus

One evening, around eight o'clock, I knelt by Shawn's wheel-chair (they removed him daily from his bed to prevent bed sores) and began to go through the "Romans Road" with him—that we are all sinners, that God has given each of us eternal life as a gift through Jesus, and that we must trust and surrender to God. I knew Shawn had fallen away from the Lord (if he ever truly knew Him) and had been living a life contrary to the gospel. I believed Shawn was still in there—in some mysterious way—and I wanted to give him the opportunity to accept Jesus as his Lord and Savior, to be connected with God, whom he had heard about his entire life. I wanted to see my son again, even if it meant in the afterlife.

As I shared the gospel with him, tears began flooding from Shawn's eyes. He was essentially weeping without expression, without noise. This was so much more than the tiny smile or tear we saw at the first hospital or the few tears we saw at the second. I felt that Shawn was moved in some profound way—like he had truly committed his life to Jesus.

A week or so later, around the sixty-day mark for his coma, a nurse was performing her daily duties for Shawn. Suddenly, she heard some kind of gibberish from his bed. She said it took her a second to register that the noise had come from the person who had been unresponsive for over two months.

She heard the gibberish again, this time a little louder. Shawn was talking. That's right, *talking*.

He was awake. His coma had subsided. A modern-day Lazarus, I felt God had returned Shawn from the dead.

Three different hospitals.

Three different times he cried.

When doctors suggested that it was time to remove his feeding tube, Shawn—against all odds—provided us with some signs of hope for us to hang on.

Surrendered Down the Nile

Shawn's recovery from that point was slow. He was essentially born again, both spiritually and physically.

In the first few days, his sight was as good as looking through a pinhole. His memory remained intact, but it took a while for his speech to return. His rehabilitation would take years. He'd suffered some minor long-term cognitive effects from his overdose, but miraculously returned to his full self.

Shawn has since become something of a health guru, sure to work out every day, sometimes twice, and religiously monitor his diet. He has become quite the foodie as well. He is working, and runs his nonprofit, Brinjured (brinjured.org). He shares with people the miracle God did with him. The name came from when he was working with his speech therapist when she asked him if he knew why he was in the hospital. He tried to say, "I'm brain injured," but it came out "brinjured." His nonprofit helps provide information and raise awareness about traumatic brain injuries while combatting the overdosing epidemic in the United States.

My son would add two more tattoos to go along with the *Elohim* tattoo on his chest. Inked on his forearm in Hebrew is *Jehovah Rapha*, which means "God heals." Etched across his ribs is *Jehovah Jireh*, which means "God provides." The verse Shawn always quotes when sharing his story is 1 Peter 2:9, "I can now proclaim the excellencies of God, who called me out of darkness into His marvelous light."

When I hear Moses's origin story, I can't help but think of Shawn.

At the time of Moses's birth, Pharaoh had ordered the killing of every Hebrew boy, leading Moses's mother to desperately place her son in a basket and send him floating down the Nile River, with the hopes he would be found. In a strange turn of events, Egyptian nobles discovered the boy in the basket, and Pharaoh's daughter raised Moses. The daughter of the very person, Pharaoh, who had ordered the brutal massacre, became his surrogate mother.

We, too, had to surrender our son to God, enter an entirely helpless state, and, in a sense, even say goodbye. His life was no longer in our hands. If Marilyn and I are honest with ourselves, it never was. Shawn had always belonged to God.

I'll never know why Shawn came out of his coma while so many others do not. We'll never know why Moses survived Pharaoh's decree while so many other Hebrew boys were brutally massacred. But I do know this: God continues to shine a light in the darkness in a broken world where people have the free will to make life-altering mistakes and do terrible things. As John 1:3-5 says, "Through him all things were made; without him nothing was made that has been made. In him was life, and that life was the light of all mankind. The light shines in the darkness, and the darkness has not overcome it."

To find *true* purpose and become participators in the divine force of restorative justice, I'm convinced that we must all allow ourselves to be rescued. No, we should not do something foolish like my son did, who put his life at risk with his decision-making. And no, hopefully, our families don't find themselves in a situation like Moses's mother did, desperately seeking refuge for her son from a violent tyrant. But we all must enter into that vulnerability nonetheless. That space where we are open to where God might take us down the river of our lives, even if it is toward a most unlikely place. That space where we are humbled. That space where we are completely dependent on God to show up.

A young Hollywood director, Brian Ivie, created a twenty-minute film in 2015 about Shawn's miraculous healing (it's free to watch at shawnmiracle.com). It has been viewed over a million times and is in five different languages. Shawn's miraculous recovery propelled him forward in new ways; but also impacted those who witnessed it first-hand. That included myself.

As Shawn slowly regained his senses in the first couple months of his recovery, I felt something calling me into action. It wasn't an audible voice, but it arose from deep within my spirit.

The call was this: *I gave you your son back; now I want you to help give other children back to their families.*

What did that mean? I'd soon find out.

2
BORN TO FIGHT

"A private faith that does not act in the face of oppression is no faith at all."
~William Wilberforce

Growing up, I had an uncle, Jerry Malone, who we called Uncle Chosh (pronounced ch-oh-sh). He had no children but treated his sister's four kids and his brother's (my dad's) three kids as if they were his own. My dad was a bit detached from our family, as many fathers were in that day. Dad was a hard worker but was obsessed with gambling. I think it's fair to say that he enjoyed being at the horse track more than at home. It was not uncommon in that day for fathers to beat the daylights out of their kids—my dad was no different. Sometimes, it was hard to tell whether we were being disciplined or were merely targets of his anger, as he beat us with a switch, belt, board, or hose while cursing like a sailor and verbally berating my brother and me.

Uncle Chosh stepped in and ensured that we all felt supported and loved by a father-like figure. He spoiled us and was always present, especially at everyone's sporting events. What broke my heart growing up was that my uncle was always ridiculed. He was a Jefferson County judge who weighed almost four hundred pounds. It pained me that people made fun of him for something as shallow as how he looked. He had given his life to help people and serve our community. But people sometimes caricatured him instead of experiencing his loving heart and brilliant mind.

One day, I was playing shortstop at Valley Sports Little League in Pleasure Ridge Park, a suburb of Louisville, Kentucky, when I noticed three kids, probably young teenagers, in the bleachers making fun of my uncle. I was maybe nine or ten years old. I prayed to God, "Don't let them leave before this game ends." I kept an eye on them throughout the game. Their teasing continued. My uncle ignored them.

In the last inning, they moved behind the outfield fence. When the final strike was pitched, I remember throwing down my glove and darting through the outfield toward the bullies as fast as I could. I hopped the fence and tried to fight all three of them at once. A couple of them must've seen the rage in my eyes because they ran away, even though all three could have possibly given me a beating. I think I landed a couple of good punches, though.

You could say that was my first big fight, my first time standing up for justice, my first time standing up for what was "right" or, to use a Biblical word, *righteous*.

Another time, I was in my first-grade class at Holy Name taking a test when one of my classmates, Leo, kept leaning over and trying to cheat off me. I told him to stop, but he ignored me. He eventually got frustrated and knocked my test off my desk onto the ground. I have no idea where the teacher, a nun, was at the time or how she didn't hear the commotion.

Leo leaned over to pick up my test, hoping to glimpse more of my answers. As he leaned over, I kicked him as hard as I could in the forehead. Leo began screaming and crying. Suddenly, the nun could hear again. I was sent to the principal, and then sent home. We lived in the Arcade Apartments, considered by many to be "the projects." My dad spanked me relentlessly.

One thing is certain about Dad: he made me tough. One time, Dad was beating me and my brother, Kyle, who was a year and a half younger than me. He verbally berated us with each whipping, as his voice heightened with every smack until he was letting out blood-curdling screams of unprocessed rage. His anger was so over-the-top and absurd that my brother and I started laughing hysterically. It was truly maniacal. Our laughter made Dad even more angry, which made him swing harder—which made us laugh even harder—and so on. He eventually got tired and stopped. Interestingly, though, my dad never laid a hand on my sister, Kelly.

All that to say, pain never scared me. As I grew older, making my way through Bishop David High School and then the University of Louisville, I never retreated from a fight. I always escalated and engaged. Before I found Jesus, or, better said, before Jesus found me, I fought for the sake of fighting, feeling invincible. I liked the rush. I enjoyed looking and feeling tough.

The adrenaline, the excitement—it felt like my body became alive.

I've been sucker punched at bars. I've been kicked out of fraternities and sororities. I guess I probably had a chip on my shoulder. I always felt I was fighting an uphill battle. I was small, the underdog—but, not in my mind.

My preferred person to fight was anyone willing. I had all this pent-up emotion inside to prove myself one way or another. I poured it into baseball and, when that wasn't enough, took it out on others. My University of Louisville roommate and baseball teammate, Glen Sterchi, liked to fight, too. We were bad news.

I was searching, trying to figure things out—lost.

Today's Fight

In 2018, we opened a safe home in Florida for boys who had been trafficked. It was called the USIAHT Hero House.

One of the boys, let's call him Billy, was lured into trafficking by two men via online video gaming in St. Petersburg, Florida. The boy met the men at their wedding three weeks before when he was brought there by a family member, who would also be tried as a conspirator.

The two men began "grooming" Billy through online apps and video games. "Grooming" is a word that anti-trafficking activists use to describe tactics used to manipulate, gain access, and coerce victims into abuse. Billy began organically sharing more of his life with these two men the more he gamed with them and communicated with them via apps like Discord, Omegle, and Roblox. Their questions became more personal.

Do you like school? The answer was no.

Do you like your mom? That answer, they learned, was no.

What do you want that your mom won't let you have? The answer was a husky.

And just like that, the two predators had their "in." Predators and groomers seek to exploit fractures in the personal lives of victims—in this case, Billy's broken relationship with his mother.

They told him they would save him from having to live with his mother, that he wouldn't have to go to school, and that they would get them a husky puppy. Before Billy knew it, these men drove 140 miles to pick him up. Groomers often try to fill the family void for the victim, fulfilling their need for love and belonging, thus strengthening the victim's attachment to them. Billy was given a new phone. His digital footprint was wiped clean. He was given a new name and identity.

For the next year, Billy was kept in a trailer at a mobile home park as a sex slave, forced to sleep on the floor, as they sold him to perverts ten to fifteen, sometimes twenty times, a day.

He was told they'd kill his husky if he tried to escape.

These are the disgusting tactics of predators who exploit the vulnerabilities within a person's story—the weaknesses within a person's life—then gain emotional leverage over the person.

Recovered text messages reveal how unhappy Billy was. "I'm stressed to high hell," he once texted the men. "I don't want sex all the time."

One of his captors responded, "Which is such a shame when

such a tight group of people who love you have come into your life."

The predators employed similar online tactics with a seventeen-year-old Louisiana boy, who they drove ten hours to pick up from his rural home in the middle of the night. When Louisiana police discovered the boy's online messages, they alerted the police in St. Petersburg, Florida. Billy was found, and seven suspects were arrested.

One day at our safe home, Billy was watching television with the director of our safe home, John, when suddenly the face of one of his captors popped up in a preview of a coming news segment about the raid of their trailer. John knew he couldn't just change the channel.

"You okay?" John asked.

"He was really nice to me," Billy commented.

One time, John asked Billy why he continued sleeping on the floor, two months into his time at the safe home. "Is the bed uncomfortable? We can get you a bigger bed."

"It's just more comfortable for me to sleep on the floor," Billy said solemnly.

Time and again in our fight against human trafficking, we come face-to-face with the stark darkness of the world and the unfathomable depths of trauma. A complex trauma that would lead a young boy to say that the trafficker who enslaved him for sex was nice to him, a trauma that led Billy to continue sleeping on the floor.

If this story doesn't make you want to fight, then maybe this book isn't for you.

Perhaps you should check to make sure you still have a pulse!

The Egyptian Slavedriver

We're all fighters on some level, aren't we? We have these emotions swarming around inside us. We have ideas in our heads and dreams in our hearts. The question is: What will we do with all this energy? Will we become seized by it and react to it as my dad did, as I did? Or will we use it for the good of others?

I think we are all born to fight. There is simply too much darkness in the world to ignore. To ignore that darkness requires a great deal of cognitive dissonance.

The question is: *How* will we fight? Hopefully, with more discernment than I did throughout high school and college—not with our fists but rather our hearts, minds, and faith.

Where will we fight? Within the sphere of influence where God has placed us.

Who will we fight? Those causing undeniable harm to others and evil into the world.

What will we fight? Injustice.

I'm reminded of Moses when he killed the Egyptian guard who was beating the Hebrew slave. At that time, Moses was likely beginning to make connections to his Hebrew past, and his conscience was perhaps beginning to be stirred as he witnessed the Egyptians' enslavement of the Hebrews. Exodus 2:11-12 explains: "One day, after Moses had grown up, he went to where his people were and watched them at their hard labor. He saw an Egyptian beating a Hebrew, one of his own people. Looking this way and that and seeing no one, he killed the Egyptian and hid him in the sand."

We can almost picture Moses experiencing a rage he had not experienced before and reacting without discernment to the emotion gripping him. His conviction and passion were good. God was working on his heart and conscience. However, his reaction to that emotion led him into sin, perpetuating a cycle of violence. As he would soon find out, an eye for an eye was not the solution. *Grace* was God's way, not war. Redemptive justice was the only path forward.

How will we use our passions, convictions, and emotions to *heal* the world rather than perpetuate cycles of darkness and violence? Maybe that means marching on Washington to protest a political policy yet refusing to demonize others in the process (frequently, protests turn bitter as people get drunk on rhetoric).

Maybe that means using one's creative skills to paint something a world-changing nonprofit can auction. Maybe that means using one's leadership and networking skills to tackle a problem that has nothing to do with the "bottom line" for one's company.

Moses seems to have been a passionate person who needed God's help to direct his passion the right way: toward justice, not violence, and redemption, not retribution. An apathetic person doesn't just kill an Egyptian who is beating a Hebrew, risking his reputation and very life. His passion was misguided, resulting in violence and an attempted coverup. Still, his conversion before the burning bush invited him into a dialogue and partnership with Yahweh to harness his passion the right way.

Maybe you don't have a fighting spirit like I do, but I bet you are passionate about the cause you want to pursue. In what areas of your life do you sometimes get sidetracked or waste your God-given energy? What disciplines can you adopt that will help you harness your energy and passion correctly?

Moses would go on to find why. And, so would I. I would eventually put all my fighting energy toward something far more meaningful than petty bar fights. For a while I thought that was winning baseball championships. But I was so wrong.

3
CALLED FORTH

"Calling is not only a matter of being and doing what we are but also of becoming what we are not yet but are called by God to be."
~Os Guinness

When I was eight or nine years old, one day, my mother asked me if I wanted to go with her to church. I told her no since I was playing outside with neighborhood friends. Why would I *willingly* go to church? I only went because it was important to my parents or to see my friends. The most I ever hung around the church was when my friends and I were determined to throw a kickball through an opening in the steeple. We were eventually successful, but then we didn't have a kickball.

We sure didn't think that one through!

Mom was fine with me not going that day. But as she left for church, something strange happened. I was overcome with a sense of sadness and loneliness. I tried to play with my friends, but I couldn't stop thinking about going to church. I suddenly realized that I really wanted to go. Mom was out of sight, but my conviction was strong. I told my friends I couldn't play anymore and took off running down the street toward St. Polycarp Church in Pleasure Ridge Park.

I found Mom in a pew, and we enjoyed the Mass together. Spending time with my mother was the best for me. She was my champion, my rock.

Another time, in fourth grade, I remember my teacher, Sister Roberta Ann, announcing to our class that we had a free period to go outside and play on the playground or go to church. I felt it again, that same familiar call. Within me existed a tension between wanting to play at "second recess"—which, as you might remember, was one of the biggest deals in grade school—or spending time with God, though I had no idea who God was. A tension within me seemed to rattle me, one that I now understand to be a conflict between "self" and "soul." Which would I choose?

I went to church.

I sat alone in a wooden pew while everyone else went to the playground.

I did not know why I was there or what I was supposed to do, but I somehow understood deep in my bones that I was in the right place. I now believe that I was seeking a deeper understanding of what life was all about. It's as though I knew there was *something* better, something greater, something bigger than my own life out there somewhere. I was young and knew nothing, yet I longed to know God and do what God wanted me to do.

Citizens of Heaven

Augustine famously said, "Our heart is restless until it rests in You."

Whatever pull I may have felt toward God in my youth became suppressed by selfish ambitions in high school and college. My heart remained restless. But never did it rest in God. Instead, my life was centered around pleasure. All I cared about was baseball, fighting, and sex, probably in that order. All of these avenues provided ego boosts I had never before experienced. Getting drunk and high in the dorms was a common occurrence. But doing so while getting naked and creating a slip-and-slide in the dormitory halls was chaos. Or while stripping down on a baseball trip (why were we always taking off our clothes?) at the hotel and hanging from luggage carts as our teammates sped us down the hallway.

My nickname on campus at the University of Louisville was "Hog," partially because I worked hard on the baseball field and because I was always consuming whatever made me feel good—you know, *hogging* things for myself. My friend, fellow high school and college teammate Brandon Chesser, first called me "Hog" in high school. There are too many stories to count that led to that nickname. Pleasure was my core motive. But no matter how much attention I received through baseball, or from a "heroic" fraternity fight, or from an attractive woman, I was left feeling emptier than before. I was caught in a spiral that I knew was not working for me.

What are you pursuing at all costs, thinking it will fulfill you? What do you tend to idolize? What distractions of the self deter you from listening to your soul? Are you a citizen of this earth or a citizen of heaven? To be a citizen of heaven is to see our relationship and connection with Jesus as the central aspect of our lives. We serve the Lord above all else. Our citizenship coveys the values and ideals we hold as inhabitants of this heavenly kingdom. We realize that this earthly world is not our home. I was undoubtedly a citizen of the earth during those days. Heaven was the last thing on my mind.

Moses on the Run

Moses's unlikely journey—from the Nile to the palace—resulted in being raised by some of the most powerful people in society. They were the very people who enslaved the Hebrews and oppressed Moses's biological family. Moses was now part of the elite inner circle. He had it all. But it seems that the more he learned about his background and Hebrew roots, the more his conscience worked on him. Just as Pharaoh's daughter found the baby Moses in a basket, God found Moses and took him in.

When Moses fled to Midian after killing the Egyptian guard,

his soul searched for something. I think we can assume that something within Moses was deeply unsettled. As part of the Egyptian elite, did Moses, too, live a life centered around pleasure and luxury that eventually led to his breaking point? Did he know that what he saw around him in the enslavement of the Israelites was wrong but tried to suppress his conscience? How empty did Moses feel at that time for him to snap in that way and take another man's life?

I don't encourage you to do what Moses did to that Egyptian, but I do suggest you do what Moses did in the fallout. *Run.* Run from what you know is wrong toward what you know is right, even if into the abyss. Do what I did that day when Mom asked me if I wanted to go to church, and I said no. Just. Run.

Run away from the empty pleasure you have built your life around. Run toward truth. Run away from your comfortable way of life. Run into the emptiness instead of always trying to fill it. Run away from your selfishness and toward the call of the soul.

4
SPOTLIGHT

"And you will know the truth, and the truth will set you free."
-John 8:32

One afternoon, my family and I decided to watch the 2015 film *Spotlight*, which tells the story of *The Boston Globe's* "Spotlight" investigative team—the oldest investigative journalism unit in the United States. That team uncovered a pattern of sexual abuse by Catholic priests in Massachusetts and decades of coverup by the Boston Archdiocese. Of course, unfortunately, the local pattern of abuse that the Spotlight team reported turned out to be part of a larger pattern that had been unfolding in churches worldwide—one of the great and deserved stains on Christianity today, particularly Catholicism.

When my family and I watched *Spotlight* that afternoon in a Los Angeles theatre, my kids were surprised to see me suddenly burst into uncontrollable tears. My wife knew why, but my children did not.

"What was that about?" Shannon and Shawn prodded on the drive home.

I took a deep breath and asked God for the courage to share this hurt, pain, and sadness. Then, I told them about what had happened to me.

My experiences with religion in my youth were mostly negative. The nuns at my school were mean. *Really* mean. They would beat us with rulers, chalk erasers, paddles, and their hands, which was not uncommon during that day. They were angry, demeaning, and seemed to hate their lives as much as they seemed to hate us. Joy was nowhere to be found. Why be a Christian anyway?

There was one nun, however, who would play football with us at recess. I think her name was Sister Laurita, my third-grade teacher. She was personable, brilliant, attractive, athletic, and genuinely wanted to connect with the boys and girls she taught. I remember thinking that a nun out there competing with us and high-fiving us after big plays was pretty cool. She was a beacon of light for me at a time when anything connected to religion seemed rigid and unenjoyable. She had a different kind of faith— there was a true joy about her that made each of us feel loved by her and God.

My childhood experiences with priests at our parish followed a similar trend to the nuns. The priests were joyless, cold, and, yes, weird. Before I go any further, you should know this about small midwestern and southern communities during the Sixties and Seventies. In many people's minds, the church could do no wrong. Families freely trusted their sons and daughters to the care of nuns at the school and priests at the parish. This happened before the Catholic Church's sexual abuse scandal was revealed, long before the "Me Too" movement, long before there was widespread talk about consent, or, shockingly, age of consent. Many parents did not talk to their kids about sex, healthy relationships, etc. Neighborhoods like ours sometimes lived in denial of the darkness in the world. They didn't think they needed to fight. They didn't know that they needed to scout the enemy.

This was also at a time when American people generally trusted our institutions, whether it be the government, schools, or churches. That sentiment began to shift during and after the Vietnam War. In a small midwestern community like ours, parents handed their children over to the care of the local Catholic school and church, believing that was the best thing they could do for their children's development and faith.

As an altar boy, I had a priest who, several times, kissed all over my neck before or after Mass, as I had seen him do to other altar boys. It's not like his actions were a secret, either. My friends and I thought it was weird, and it seemed to be widespread knowledge among families that this was "just the way the priest was." He was just "affectionate" in his own way.

The sentiment was, *That's kind of strange, but he's the priest, so he's on a holier level than all of us.* We were mere plebes, common village folk, needing a priest to help us get closer to God. At that time, there was no questioning his authority to be in the position he was in. After all, priests had taken a vow of celibacy. What a holy calling! Who were *we* to make such claims about someone's character? About someone's *sexuality?*

Maybe you can begin to see how these situations were swept under the rug in religious communities for decades. It takes courageous people to shine the spotlight on injustice, to fight, and scout the enemy to bring the truth to the surface.

There was one priest, however, Rev. Jim Hargadon, who seemed much like Sr. Laurita. We would get together and play racquetball. We would even sometimes go to the bar afterward and have a beer together. In my mind, all of this was equivalent to Sr. Laurita throwing the football with us at recess.

Between my senior year and college, Fr. Hargadon invited me to go on a trip with him to New Orleans. I'm not even sure what the reason for the trip was; maybe something to do with a gathering of Catholic clergy. I knew the decisions I was making during my "hog days" weren't great, but I wasn't sure why I should be a religious person. Maybe the priest could help. I decided to go.

Surprisingly, however, my trip to New Orleans was filled with partying and bar hopping with the priest. One evening—and, to this day, I struggle to find the words—it seemed like I was drugged. When the priest came into my hotel room late that night after bar hopping with him, it was as if I was completely out of my body, looking down from the ceiling at the sexual abuse that was happening, observing the scene. I don't need to go into details, but whether it was shock, alcohol, drugs, or all of the above, my body felt paralyzed as my soul observed from above. Watching what this pervert was doing to me was bizarre. I guess I forced myself to separate myself from reality. I was confused and didn't know what to think or do.

In the middle of the night, once I came to my senses, I darted from my hotel room to find a payphone. I was frantic. I was seven hundred miles from home, in a city I had never been to, with no money to get a plane or bus ticket, and trapped with a monster. My first call was not to my dad, but to Uncle Chosh.

In broken words, I told him I needed to get out of New Orleans as soon as possible. Usually, Uncle Chosh was one to ask questions and gather details. But this time, he didn't. I think he could tell by the tone of my voice that something terrible had happened. As a county judge who worked closely with law enforcement, maybe he had heard some rumors about Jim Hargadon.

"On my way," Uncle Chosh said without delay.

On my way.

Those words would become etched in my heart.

How many trafficked, abused children today are just waiting, hoping, and praying from the pit of desperation that a rescuer will say those words to them?

My uncle went straight to the airport at three o'clock in the morning and bought me a plane ticket, which you could do back then for anyone, anywhere. I hitchhiked to the airport and got the hell out of New Orleans.

Decades later, Jim Hargadon was convicted on several counts of child molestation charges. He spent the rest of his sorry life in jail.

Moses: The Ultimate Scout
As many survivors of sexual abuse will tell you—though I didn't

have the language at the time—there was a deeper aimlessness to my existence after New Orleans, some kind of fundamental fracture at the very core of my being that continued to spread the more I *reacted* to that pain. I had always been a fighter, but now my fighting escalated. I trusted no one, especially men. I had a chip on my shoulder. My goal every time I partied with my teammates on the baseball team at the University of Louisville was to either get in a fight or get laid—it was such a futile way of life. But I was lost, angry, desperately searching for something to fill the void in my heart.

I wonder what horrors Moses witnessed during the time he spent in the circle of the Egyptian elite. What atrocities did he see Pharaoh and others committing in their dehumanizing of the Hebrews? Physical abuse? Verbal abuse? Sexual abuse? I wonder what accumulation of events led him to take the life of the Egyptian guard. What led to his breaking point?

Scripture doesn't answer these questions, but one thing seems unmistakable: Moses's experience in Egypt would one day propel him toward his purpose. Without knowing it, Moses was a scout. Throughout his adolescent and early adult life, he scouted the "enemy" by being immersed in Egyptian culture.

His upbringing was likely very nuanced. Pharaoh's daughter had to have known Moses was a Hebrew boy whom Pharaoh had ordered killed, but she rescued him anyway. She raised him and, we can assume, loved him. Moses would not have lived had it not been for Pharaoh's daughter. Then again, Moses wouldn't have been surrendered down the Nile had it not been for her father. Nonetheless, Pharaoh's daughter responded to the call. She listened to her loving motherly instincts, did what she did not have to do, and took Moses in.

Think about it. Without Pharaoh's daughter, there is no Exodus.

However, this upbringing inside the walls of those who oppressed and enslaved the Hebrews *also* led to Moses likely witnessing firsthand the force of darkness. He was probably surrounded by royals who used their wealth and power to perse-cute and exploit the Hebrews. One may wonder if *he* ever partook in this persecution of his people. Or if he was treated poorly by people who knew who he actually was.

Nonetheless, somehow, some way, Moses was brought to his breaking point. The weight of the darkness led to an outburst. God was not done with him. God would use him in a profound way, perhaps divinely chosen *because* of his deep understanding of the Egyptian way of life.

Without downplaying the horrors of trauma and the sheer weight of the darkness people experience, I tend to believe that God can use the brokenness in our own stories to help heal frac-tures in the stories of others.

After the priest's abuse, I poured a lot of my unprocessed pain into baseball. I was not the most athletic ball player. I was essentially a walk-on my first year at the University of Louisville, which had a solid baseball program. I worked my tail off and, by my senior year, was named lead-off hitter and captain. Athletics provided a healthy avenue to release the rage that boiled inside me. I had two great coaches, Jim Zerilla (my first three years) and John Boles (my senior year). Coach Boles ended up managing the Florida Marlins in the Major Leagues.

This was the very beginning, I guess, of what would become my life's story: taking the pain inside me and using it to propel me forward. This aspect of my life—*sports*—was an avenue where I transformed my pain into hard work. As I reflect on what happened to me in New Orleans and in my hometown parish, I suppose I would have had every right to lose hope or give up. But, I did not give up. Something inside me made me feel that life would improve and that good things were ahead. I truly believed the words my Mom always said to me: that I could be something, that I *would* be somebody someday. In a sense, because I loved baseball and competing, it would become the very trajectory of my life: to take my frustrations and pour them into something meaningful.

Never could I have imagined that my experience in New Orleans and in the Catholic Church would one day be the impetus for my purpose, my call, my pursuit of justice. I never could have imagined that I would one day become an activist for ending child sex trafficking.

An activist is a person who campaigns for change and uses decisive actions in support of justice or opposition to injustice. They act to make changes in society toward a greater good. They advocate for a cause.

Moses was an activist. Jesus was an activist.

As playwright and novelist Thornton Wilder once wrote, "Without your wound where would your power be?" Daring to believe that our lives are not over when something terrible happens to us (even if it feels that way) has a lot of psychological and practical benefits. Jesus Christ exemplified this on the cross and, in doing so, showed us the way. His horrific, excruciating crucifixion in front of all his loved ones on that terrible afternoon turned out to be wounds that saved the world. Through suffering, he modeled for us all how to serve.

In my advocacy work, I hope to echo what my Uncle Chosh told me almost five decades ago and what John at the safe house essentially says anytime he gets a call about another trafficked boy needing safety and refuge from the world's darkness.

On my way.

5
SEARCHING FOR SOMETHING

*"There is a God-shaped vacuum in the heart of each man which
cannot be satisfied by any created thing but only by God the
Creator, made known through Jesus Christ."*
~Blaise Pascal

My lifestyle in college brought me to a dead-end. No amount of sex or fighting was enough to quench my soul's deepest desires.

So, I embarked upon a spiritual search.

Though I turned my back on Catholicism after the New Orleans incident, I did not give up on spirituality. Somehow, in my college lifestyle of fighting and partying—while spiritually searching in the shadows—I was saved, born again, and transformed into right standing with God through Jesus.

My entry point was reading *The Power of Positive Thinking* by Dr. Norman Vincent Peale and encountering Scripture in a new and impactful way. Attending Mass had always been bland and ritualistic to me. However, in Dr. Peale's book, I remember making the connection that Scripture could be personal and directly applicable to my situation. Until then, I had all this head knowledge about God—through attending Mass weekly, being educated in the Catholic school system, going through catechism and confirmation—but my heart was untouched. I knew stories from the Christian tradition but had never allowed them to stir my heart. I didn't understand the gospel's significance —what Jesus actually did. I knew I was lost, broken, messed up, and acting immature, but I wasn't sure what to do about it.

Dr. Peale's book inspired me to buy a Bible, and I began scouring the pages that contain those ancient words. That was the start of a deeper awareness for me. A hunger for God began to develop in my soul. The Bible was exposing me to a truth I had never before encountered. I started listening to sermons on tape. Dr. John MacArthur was my favorite Bible teacher (strangely enough, he would one day become a dear friend of mine). His love for the Word and his expository teaching fed my soul. It's not like I stopped all the toxic things in my lifestyle cold turkey—I remember reading the Word while drinking two or three beers in my dorm room!—but my priorities were shifting. I replaced partying with reading my Bible in my dorm room bed, searching to know who God is, and wanting to be in His presence. I'm not so sure if the beers helped with this.

I began attending 9th & O Baptist Church, located close to Churchill Downs, less than a mile from Holy Name Catholic Church, where I was raised. It was a fire-and-brimstone church that preached about damnation every Sunday, often waging war on the racetrack across the street and the gambling that flourished there. However, the emotion and structure were just what I needed at the time. With that emotion came conviction. With that passion, my own emotions had an outlet.

So, I became a Jesus freak. I started carrying my Bible around campus. My nickname went from "Hog" to "Holy Hog." I was devouring the Word with the same passion and energy with which I had pursued pleasure and affection. I was filling the hole—the void of what I had left behind—with my new, transformed life.

Slowly, very slowly, my fighting and hookup energy began to be harnessed differently. Instead of partying in the evenings, I hosted Bible studies. I wondered what excellence looked like and decided it had to be centered in faith in Jesus. In leaving behind my silly, consuming desire to fight physically or to have sex, space was made within my heart and mind to invest in more meaningful fights: to fight for my teammates and school on the baseball diamond and eventually to fight for justice.

In many ways, my experience in New Orleans propelled me forward. That's right, *forward*. Yes, a priest kissed my neck when I was an altar boy. It was weird and messed up. To this day, it makes me want to puke. Yes, as a teenager, a priest coerced me down to New Orleans and took advantage of me. Reliving that experience as I write this feels almost as incomprehensible as it did then.

But I have what might be described as an "athlete's approach" to life—I'm determined to use *everything* to make me better, to propel me forward. I'm hesitant to label what I experienced with that priest as a trauma. I know that must sound crazy, but in my work as an activist who fights child sex trafficking, I see children and adults dealing with much more horrific circumstances. You gain some perspective about life when you work with children who, at five or six years old, are raped ten or fifteen times a day, or realize that the largest seller of pornography is child pornography.

How messed up of a world—*of a country*—do we live in?

Writing this book, though, has forced me to slow down and think about that young Kevin Malone who was so hungry to know God—who left his friends to sprint toward the church and catch up with his mother, who skipped a free period to play outside and instead sat in that quiet church alone—but then was taken advantage of by the very people who so many people in our community trusted. How many other children did Fr. Jim Hargadon abuse? How many people did he lure in through his spiritual position, only to guilt them (or drug them) into unspeakable situations? How many people could not bounce back because the trauma was too much to bear? The effects of abuse are infinitely complex. There is no formula for healing. But there is a refuge: Jesus Christ, who entered fully into our human suffering.

Just because my athlete's approach to life allowed me to put my head down and focus on new things, my intention is not to encourage you to bypass your grief. Just because I turned the page quickly after those experiences in my youth doesn't mean you should. I'm no therapist, but I know from my work in human trafficking that any form of abuse—sexual, physical, emotional, or verbal—can severely alter someone's mentality and even their personality. There is no such thing as minor abuse—any abuse is major abuse. I have an unusual ability to compartmentalize and focus on the future. That probably helps me not get discouraged or burnt out in the intensity of the activism I do today, but maybe that didn't serve me well when it came to truly grieving some of these abuses by spiritual guides in my life whom I should have been able to trust.

However, as my family saw that day watching *Spotlight*, the wound is always there. It never goes away. Healing is a lifelong journey. I encourage you to do the hard inner work to move through your pain so that you don't become or remain a victim. Becoming a thriving survivor is the best way to get revenge on those who wronged you. I'm determined to take what I've experienced in life—even the most painful moments, perhaps *especially* the most painful moments—and use them for the good of others, to help lead others to know Jesus as their Lord and Savior.

Searching Our Stories

We are all like Moses; we must become aware of how our journeys have unfolded and what has happened to us. At some point or another, all of us, must introspectively evaluate the people and situations that made us who we are, both positive and negative.

Moses, as we can imagine, had a lot to uncover about his past if he wanted to discover the truth of who he was, to lead an authentic life and to find his purpose. We are again left to our imaginations as to what this journey would have been like for him. In Exodus 2:10, Pharaoh's daughter is pulling baby Moses from a basket out of the water, and in Exodus 2:11, just one verse later, we're told that Moses is grown up. In the very next verse, Exodus 2:12, Moses kills the Egyptian who is beating the Hebrew slave.

Again, what led to this radical transition, exactly? Was Moses himself treated as "less than" or "other" by those in his own family because they knew he was a Hebrew? Was this perhaps what led to his sympathy for the Hebrew slaves, the fact that *he* faced discrimination and abuse? Or did *he* take advantage of Hebrew slaves because of his upbringing with the Egyptian elite? Did his conscience create within him a sense of guilt and regret?

In Dreamworks' 1998 film *Prince of Egypt*, the writers imaginatively painted a scene of the veil slowly being pulled back for Moses. Growing up privileged in the palace and never questioning his identity, then accidentally running into his biological siblings, Miriam and Aaron, and being confronted about who he really is. Having a dream about Pharaoh's genocide of Hebrew male infants from which Moses narrowly escaped, finding hieroglyphs in the palace detailing the massacre, and finally gaining the courage to ask Pharaoh and his mother about his true identity and even confront his surrogate father about the genocide.

Dreamworks storytelling was creative license, but it definitely gets your imagination spinning. One thing that seems undebatable to me about Moses's development is that having been immersed in Egyptian culture, he would have witnessed firsthand the terrible treatment of the Israelites and the abuses the Hebrew people suffered. No matter, it seems likely that a culmination of events led Moses to his boiling point when he killed the Egyptian and fled Pharaoh's wrath. Moses became a man on the run without an identity, or perhaps a conflicted man seeking an identity in God.

Perhaps you have felt similarly. Maybe you've asked yourself the questions, "Who am I?" or "What am I to do?" or "What is my purpose?" Slowing down to evaluate some of the experiences that shaped my heart for justice and activism has helped me realize that I might be fighting human trafficking today, partially because of my own story. One of my life verses is Genesis 50:20, when Joseph—reunited with his brothers who had betrayed him years before and had him sold into slavery—says to them, "You intended to harm me, but God intended it for good to accomplish what is now being done, the saving of many lives."

Have you ever considered how what your enemies intended for harm could now be used to save lives? Welcome to the journey of both healing and purpose.

6

NEW LIFE

"It's not about you. The purpose of your life is far greater than your own personal fulfillment, your peace of mind, or even your happiness. It's far greater than your family, your career, or even your wildest dreams and ambitions. If you want to know why you were placed on this planet, you must begin with God."
~ Rick Warren

My conversion set me on a new path, one I could never have expected.

After my senior season at the University of Louisville, I took a winding country road south into the hills of Kentucky, parked in the middle of nowhere, and camped in the woods. I brought nothing but bottles of water. For three straight days I fasted in the forest, contemplating my future. Why fast? Fasting is the temporary renunciation of something good, like food, in order to intensify the need for something greater—God! I knew my future was in God's hands. I did not want to leave behind my dream of playing professional baseball, but I knew that would depend on whether or not I would get drafted by a team. I was thinking about what's next. Could it be ministry?

Much to my surprise, I was selected in the *thirty-fifth* round of the MLB Draft by the Cleveland Indians. You read that correctly, the thirty-fifth round. I bet you didn't even know that the MLB had that many rounds in their draft. I'm thankful that my college coach, John Boles, a future manager of the Florida Marlins, put in a good word for me.

I was to report to Batavia, New York, to play in the New York-Penn League, which was a Single A, short-season rookie league. I was the lead-off hitter for Batavia, and was becoming something of a fan favorite because I enjoyed chatting with the regulars before and after the games. I wasn't sure how long my professional baseball journey would last, and I was determined to enjoy all of it.

An hour before the first game in our series against Auburn, my manager called me into his office. "Son, you've been loaned to Auburn," he grunted.

"Today?" I said, baffled. "But we're playing Auburn."

"Clean out your locker and go to the visitor's locker room. They'll take care of you from there."

That evening, I led off for Auburn, and I think our fans genuinely thought I had put on the wrong jersey. *What is Malone doing?*

I had a decent season but was released in the offseason. At that level, organizations were looking for standout rookies who had mysteriously fallen in the draft the year before; that way, those players would be invited to Spring Training the following season and potentially be developed as an MLB prospect. I had not stood out enough.

That offseason, I worked at a baseball school operated by three Christian brothers who had long, successful careers in the MLB. I started training with them while helping them host youth baseball camps in Winter Haven, Florida. They knew of my college career and said they would leverage their connections to get me into Spring Training with an MLB organization. However, when Spring Training came, no connection had been made. They had not even tried.

This was the first of many times that a Christian would promise something and then, without an honest discussion, fail to do what was promised. Been there before? Duped by someone else's faith and professed integrity? I was beginning to see that Christian faith was not always as it seemed—those brothers (and the church we were attending) would twist and distort Bible verses to justify things like materialism and other forms of idolatry.

"I have to go find an opportunity if you aren't going to keep your word," I told them. I packed my van and drove to St. Petersburg, where the New York Mets had just begun Spring Training. The Mets would eventually invite me to their minor league training camp and extended Spring Training camp, where I shared the field with excellent players such as Darryl Strawberry and Kevin Mitchell, who had just been drafted out of high school. They had a slew of young talent in their minor league system, and I could see the writing on the wall: there was no future for me in their farm system. I decided to swing for the fences and proposed that I be moved from the extended spring team to a full-season A-ball team.

"I need to go to the next level," I told my extended Spring Training manager. It was worth a shot., However, the next day I showed up at practice, and discovered that my locker was cleaned out. I got an answer, but not the one I was hoping for. I realized that my dream of playing pro baseball had ended.

I returned to Louisville and signed with the Kentucky Bourbons, a professional softball team. I was thrilled to still be on the diamond—and getting paid for it!—but began thinking seriously about my future, which I now expected to unfold outside of baseball. I returned to the idea of ministry, that notion that had called to me during my three-day retreat in the woods before the MLB Draft.

I would describe my faith during my stint in minor league ball as hungry but frantic. I was a new believer who continued to dive into the Word, even if it went over my head. But I was still living pretty crazy, caught up at times in pleasure-seeking that consumed so many single athletes. Amidst all this, I was still an unashamed Jesus freak! I probably looked like such a hypocrite. Nonetheless, I could sense that God was calling me further into His loving arms. I knew He wanted me to learn much more about His Son.

Surrendering my baseball career to God was not a dead end but a turning point.

One and Only

I decided to explore pursuing a ministry degree while coaching baseball. I was connected to some folks in the Liberty University baseball program, but no coaching opportunities were available. I learned about Ron Bishop, the athletic director at Tennessee Temple University. I felt magnetically drawn to studying the Bible in an academic setting while coaching the university's baseball team. My Catholic family was suspicious that I was going to a Baptist college, but I was determined to learn more about the Bible.

Tennessee Temple University (and its seminary) was an ultra-conservative place but ended up being perfect for me at that time. I needed guidelines, boundaries, and structure. I needed things that were off-limits to stay focused on spiritual growth without being distracted by my selfishness. I needed to be quarantined, in a sense, so that I could detach entirely from the bad habits I had developed during my "hog days" in college.

At Temple, I was offered the assistant baseball coach position under head baseball coach John Zeller (whom everyone called "Z"), who would become instrumental in my life. Z let his Christian faith guide his relationship with his spouse. Z was a personable and energetic coach his players loved, and he modeled being in a committed relationship anchored in faith. I realized I had gotten this aspect of my life all wrong. But, rather than beating myself up, I strongly desired to be in a Christ-centered relationship.

In chapel one day (we had to attend chapel three times a week at Tennessee Temple), I saw a beautiful young lady who I would find out was named Marilyn. Decades later, I still get emotional writing about this story. When I saw her, she radiated with an otherworldly kind of glow as though the Holy Spirit was resting upon her. This effect may have been a trick of the light in the chapel or my imagination, but it left a lasting impression.

I eventually met Marilyn through my athletic director's secretary, who was acquainted with her. We went on our first date and had what I thought was a wonderful conversation over a nice dinner in Chattanooga, Tennessee. But then she disappeared for six months. I wondered what I had said wrong. I wondered if she could see straight through me and caught a glimpse of who I had once been.

She had experienced her own difficulties with men and did not trust them. Marilyn's older sister Nancy was experiencing marriage challenges, and her soon-to-be ex-husband left a bad taste in her mouth about men. Because of that situation, Marilyn wasn't interested in getting to know me any better. She eventually came back around, decided to give me a shot, and we began to date.

Our relationship was unlike any I had ever had. I don't think I had ever been in a relationship that wasn't driven by purely physical components. As a result, my past relationships would always fizzle out because they lacked depth and friendship. Not with Marilyn.

Marilyn and I read the Bible together. We prayed together. We attended church and chapel together and discussed the sermons we heard. We prioritized faith, honesty, and emotional vulnerability. We'd spend hours on the phone talking when we weren't together. It was important for us to know each other completely.

Perhaps most impactful was that we had Z and his wife, Katie, to look up to. Actually, Z would one day be in our wedding. There is no question that we modeled our relationships after theirs. Their commitment, trust, joy, and grounding in their Christian faith radiated from their relationship. We spent a lot of time with them at their house, attended church with them every Sunday morning and Wednesday night, and went on countless double dates. Being a little older than us and deep into their marriage, they unintentionally mentored us.

I fell more and more in love with Marilyn during my first year in seminary, her senior year of undergrad. She was a mature Christian, light years ahead of me in faith and understanding of scripture. She was brilliant and curious. As easy-going and go-with-the-flow as she was, she also had strong principles and unshakable ethics. She knew what she wanted. She didn't play games.

That summer, while playing pro softball for the Kentucky Bourbons—the 1981 World Champions of Professional Softball!—the father of one of my teammates hired me to work construction and help build a McDonald's in Louisville from the ground up.

I used the money to buy an engagement ring. I found everything I was looking for in Marilyn, and wasn't letting this one get away.

Within a year of beginning to date, Marilyn and I were married on February 19, 1983, at 9th & O Baptist Church in Louisville. The reception was in the gymnasium at St. Polycarp Catholic Church, where our family and friends could drink bourbon or beer, or both. Of course, my mom decorated the gymnasium beautifully with her special, loving touch.

Foreigner in a Foreign Land

Merely one verse after reading that Moses fled to Midian after killing the Egyptian, we read that he encountered the seven daughters of a priest near a well in Midian. As they fetched water from a well for their father's flock, a group of troublesome shepherds tried to drive them away, but Moses intervened. Next thing we know, the priest is giving away his daughter Zipporah to Moses to be married.

And I thought that Marilyn and I had moved fast!

We're told in Exodus 2:22 that Moses and Zipporah had a son they named Gershom, which means, "I have become a foreigner in a foreign land."

I can relate to this notion of being a foreigner in a foreign land. The culture at Tennessee Temple was unlike anything I had ever experienced before. We had a curfew, chapel three times a week, separate dorms for boys and girls, and girls had to wear long skirts (no shorts, no pants, no short skirts). My free time was spent going on walks around campus with Marilyn, studying the Bible, and developing relationships with the guys on the baseball team. It was as if I was living a completely different life— as if I had truly been born again. Sometimes, it was shocking to compare my life at the University of Louisville to my life at Tennessee Temple. Yet, no matter how strange I felt in this strange new land, where the emphasis was on getting to know God and growing in my relationship with Jesus Christ, I somehow knew I was right where I needed to be.

This is the nature of finding one's purpose. You usually don't find it by being comfortable; by doing what you've always done. When Paul uses the word "repent" in the New Testament, he means making a complete 180-degree turn in one's life. Moses did that when he fled from Egypt to Midian. He started all over. Yes, he did so out of necessity due to killing the Egyptian guard. But, by fleeing to Midian, he had gone from the penthouse to the outhouse.

Though the narrative in Exodus 2 moves quickly, some scholars believe that Moses spent up to forty years in the desert land of Midian before meeting his future wife, which is a lesson in itself. Being a foreigner in a foreign land is not easy. It takes time. Sometimes, your purpose doesn't become apparent right away. God has to work on your heart first. He has to quarantine you. He has to empty you and purify you of the sin and bad habits that prevent you from living a spiritually abundant and full life (John 10:10).

A common motif in the Bible is the notion of the desert being a place of preparation and sanctification. When Jesus fasted in the desert for forty days and forty nights, Satan tempted him in every way—yet, he never wavered from his identity as God's beloved and chosen one. The number forty is seen in the Bible as a period of trial, of testing in order to be cleansed or refined and protected. Why did Jesus spend forty days in the wilderness? The Scriptures indicate that Jesus had proven that he was ready for his purpose after those forty days and nights in the desert.

Leave Egypt, my friends. Flee toward Midian. Make your home in the desert. Repent. Make a complete 180-degree turn. Don't be afraid to become a foreigner in a foreign land.

7
THE CLIMB

"Passion is the degree of difficulty we are willing to endure to accomplish the goal."
~Louis Giglio

As I washed a line of golf carts in the Isla Del Sol Country Club parking lot in St. Pete Beach, Florida, I wondered what the heck I was going to do with my life. I was twenty-five years old, newly married, and working as an "assistant pro" at a golf course, which meant that I managed the pro shop, washed golf carts, and gave lessons to beginners who couldn't tell how little I knew about golf. My dreams of playing professional baseball were officially over.

I had decided not to complete my seminary degree, as I had received a job offer to teach at the Jim Rice Baseball School in St. Petersburg. I figured I could always return to seminary, but wanted to stay connected to baseball as long as possible. The position didn't pay much, but my job at the golf course made a little extra cash. Marilyn, who majored in business administration, worked as a front office manager for a dental office. We were a young couple, living paycheck to paycheck, but happy and in love!

Neither of us could have imagined where our lives would soon be heading.

I knew a couple of baseball scouts. One in particular, Lou Snipp, coached me for one semester at the University of Louisville. Lou taught me many aspects of how to think and play the game. Most importantly, he taught me how to believe in myself. I may have always come across as confident in college, but my fighting was always about proving myself. Lou instilled confidence in me. If he believed in me, then I could believe in myself.

I contacted Lou, and he connected me to the East Coast supervisor for the California Angels, Al Goldis. Al interviewed me and offered me a job as a low-level scout, overseeing the Los Angeles area, making $12,000 a year, which was big money for a broke guy washing golf carts!

I will go deeper into some of the lessons I learned as a scout in Major League Baseball—hence, the title of this book—throughout Part II, but here is a brief overview of what happened.

My rise in the ranks of Major League Baseball is as inconceivable to me now as it was then. After spending three years in the Southern California scouting role for the Angels, I had a similar role with the Montreal Expos for a year. My job with both was to scout every high school, junior college, and college within my territory. After the June draft, I would coach part of the season with a rookie league team, and scouting minor and major league teams.

In 1989, scouting director Terry Ryan gave me a big promotion (and a move to St. Petersburg, Florida) as the East Coast Supervisor for the Minnesota Twins. My job was to evaluate top East Coast and Latin America prospects, and I was also assigned to scout the Atlanta Braves for the last eighteen games of the 1991 regular season. (The Twins did play the Braves in the World Series that year.)

My scouting report was approximately two hundred pages long. That helped land me Scouting Director and Assistant General Manager positions with the Expos. Two years later, I was promoted to General Manager.

It's all wild to reflect upon. Seven years before, I was washing golf carts.

Warped Priorities

People often ask me if some breakthrough helped me rise through the ranks, like *Moneyball's* Billy Beane or Paul DePodesta, the Oakland A's masterminds credited with popularizing sabermetrics: using statistical analysis to evaluate baseball players. I can't say there was. It was the grace of God, drive, determination, the chip on my shoulder, and the people who provided me various opportunities to prove myself.

Maybe what helped separate me from others was that I'd sacrifice anything and everything to win. For example, most scouts would go to see one game a day. I would often go to an early practice, see the start of one game, and then hurry across town to see the end of another game. On off days, I'd go to team practices and even watch the workouts, trying to figure out a player's attitude, desire, and work ethic—what we scouts called "makeup."

But the situation got even crazier.

Our Expos scouting and player development program gained a reputation for its strong culture. In Montreal, these departments worked closely together, whereas, at many organizations, they scapegoated one another. Player development usually blamed scouting for not getting them the right guys, and scouting usually blamed player development for not doing what they needed to do to help players develop. Our two departments strengthened and complemented one another. We understood that culture was the only way we would have a chance at winning. We had the smallest payroll in baseball, which seemed like a minor league team payroll. Because of this, we knew it would take us three or four years of developing young players who weren't yet receiving superstar salaries to build a championship team.

The 1994 season was that year for us. We were locked and loaded. Two-thirds of the way through the season, we had the best record in baseball (74-40), but the MLB players' strike suddenly ended our World Series hopes. *Sporting News* named me MLB GM of the Year, but I didn't care. I had my sights on helping bring the Expos their first World Series title.

I was tasked in the offseason with orchestrating a "fire sale" because we could no longer afford the guys who had burst into the national spotlight the year before. I resigned in 1995 after the season, frustrated with ownership's unwillingness to spend money on talent and to pursue world championships.

I spent the next two and a half years as Assistant General Manager with the Baltimore Orioles. It was a special and wonderful time in my life. Working with and learning from Hall of Fame General Manager Pat Gillick in the great baseball city of Baltimore was such a tremendous blessing.

In 1996 and 1997 we made it to the American League Championship Series (ALCS), unfortunately losing to the New York Yankees and the Cleveland Indians, respectively. I still feel that our team should have won both of those World Series.

In 1996, we finished the regular season 88-74 and earned a Wild Card spot. We defeated the Cleveland Indians in the American League Divisional Series, but lost to the New York Yankees in the ALCS. We lost Game 1 in New York due to a non-fan interference call that cost us the game. The umpire failed to make the interference call and a home run was allowed. Not only did it cost us the game, but it affected the mood of the series. Interesting note, in the pregame meeting in the Yankees clubhouse, umpires specifically said that fan interference was an issue at Yankee Stadium and this was on their radar screens, but I guess those screens weren't working that day. The Yankees went on to beat the Braves in the World Series. The next year, in 1997, we won the AL East with ninety-eight wins. We beat the Seattle Mariners in the Divisional Series, but lost to the Indians in the ALCS. We lost in six games, all of which were exciting. The Indians lost to the Florida Marlins in the World Series.

My stay with the Orioles ended when I was hired in August of

1998 by the Los Angeles Dodgers to be their Executive Vice President and General Manager. The interesting aspect of leaving the Orioles was that I had a handshake agreement with Orioles team owner Peter Angelos on a three-year contract starting in 1999. My understanding is that the Dodgers contacted the Orioles (sometime after our handshake agreement) and asked for permission to interview me, and the O's granted this request. I never understood why or how that happened, but it did. My only regret was that I was interviewed for a story on my way out of town, and I said some discouraging things about Mr. Angelos's involvement with baseball operations in that previous offseason. Years later I apologized. Me and my mouth again.

Overall, I experienced lots of blessings in Baltimore, working as Pat Gillick's assistant. Though I was technically his assistant, this was an excellent professional move because of the Orioles' budget and reputation. Pat allowed me to be his co-general manager, giving me the authority to make trades and any other move that I thought would help the team—all he had to do was sign off on it. He always did.

Pat and I had skillsets and personalities that complemented one another well. He once called me an expert "rebuilder" because of my attention to detail and team-building skills. Pat had a natural ability to mentor and prepare me to oversee a massive, iconic organization. Because of him, I felt ready to eventually accept the General Manager position for the Los Angeles Dodgers.

There is one thing you will realize very quickly about me: when I'm in, I go *all in*. My wife sometimes asks me, "Why does everything have to be a competition for you?"

Because if I can't win, what's the point?

From school to athletics to my career, nothing came easy for me. I've always had to work harder than everyone else. I may not have been as talented of a player as anyone on the roster at the University of Louisville, but I knew that if I got to the field each day an hour or two before team practice, I'd be able to hold my own.

I hope this work ethic and drive—this obsessiveness with accomplishing my goals—are admirable traits. The pursuit of excellence drives me. But this determination has to be harnessed the right way. If I'm not careful, these passions and desires will consume me, and the things that are *actually* most important in life take a back seat.

Now, here is the tough part to write about.

From starting as a low-level scout for the Angels in 1985 to eventually being hired as General Manager for the Los Angeles Dodgers in 1998, those thirteen years were instrumental for my career and my family. During that time, Marilyn and I had two children: Shannon in 1987 and Shawn in 1990. As any parent will tell you, the first ten to twelve years of your children's lives are precious—the only years they depend entirely on you for comfort and care. Those are the years every parent I know seems to cherish the most. Before you know it, they are in high school with their own social schedules, then off to college on their own journeys.

I'm sad to say that I missed out on many of those precious years with my children. Baseball was my god, my idol. I've heard it said that most people spend the first half of their life *building*, maybe accumulating wealth and possessions or climbing the professional ladder. Once they realize that chasing success has left them empty—that their pursuits are futile—they will ignore that feeling of emptiness and keep trying to fill the void, or pivot and spend the second half of their life giving for others, living a life of purpose.

My story follows that trajectory. I tried never to abandon my Christian values, but the truth is that nothing was more important to me than winning—than building championship teams. As new opportunities arose as an MLB scout, I became consumed in the climb. As I made my way to the top of management, I became even more obsessed with pursuing championships.

They say that looking into the eyes of a newborn baby is like gazing into the eyes of God. Maybe I caught a quick glimpse when my children were born, but I never got a good view of heaven because I was so caught up in the world. I am embarrassed to admit that when our daughter, Shannon, was born in 1987 in Los Angeles, I was overjoyed as I held her, but in the next moment I was thinking about baseball and all that I still had to do that day and week. My mind was completely immersed in *what I did*, not in who God said that I already was—and the myriad of blessings around me that were expressions of His divine love. Shannon was born in the morning, and by that afternoon, I was back on the scouting trail, trying to find that secret weapon for the California Angels organization.

That feels absolutely crazy to write today, but it is true.

When Marilyn was pregnant with Shawn, I made sure that we scheduled a C-section just so I could block off my schedule for a few hours that day. I thought this was the *responsible* thing to do. After all, my career was *way* too "important" to be restricted to one area or "be on call" for a week straight—I was the East Coast Scouting Supervisor for the Minnesota Twins! I remember flying into St. Petersburg, Florida, for Marilyn's C-section, and by that evening, I was on another plane for work.

I would completely understand if you close this book now out of disgust,. But in my mind, I was taking care of my family financially and was therefore being a good father. As Shannon and Shawn got older, they had to attend three different grade schools in their most formative years because of my job. The most difficult for them, I'm sure, was attending school in Montreal, where they had to learn French. Marilyn felt especially lonely during those years, maybe because I wasn't home very often, and when I was home I was checked out, focused on building a championship team. They were constantly uprooted because of my job.

But again, in my mind, I was being a great father because of all the cool opportunities I provided for them financially and experientially: meeting baseball players, celebrities, and traveling to excellent places for our vacations. I know they were thankful for all these experiences, but what they wanted all along—what *every* child wants and needs—is a father who is present with them.

Marilyn was both a mother *and* father to our children during those years. She displayed the presence and attentiveness to their growth and development they needed and deserved. She often confronted me about my workaholism, but my response was always that this was the nature of working in sports. It *is* the nature of working in sports. Sports is a demanding profession that requires working many evenings, weekends, and holidays. However, plenty of God-fearing people have found balance and made a way to excel both on and off the field. There were plenty of creative things I could have done not to miss the bulk of my children's first ten years.

As I think of those times, I'm unsure if I knew *how* to be a father. I thought I was doing great—way better than my dad, at least. I didn't beat my kids. I didn't even yell at them. I provided them with cool experiences. They lived in a nice house. And when I *was* home, occasionally for the last hour before their bedtime after working a sixteen-hour day—that is, if I was in town—I was relatively present with them. I'd hold them. I'd read them a book. I'd tuck them in and pray with them. My dad sure never did stuff like that for me. When my dad wasn't aloof, he was angry. I didn't need to gamble to get my rush. I was doing *important* things, meaningful things, purposeful things—or so I thought.

I'm thankful for the work ethic my father modeled for me, but I'm afraid I also mirrored some of his disconnectedness from what is *most* important in life. My advice to all fathers is that your spouse and children should *always* be more important than your job or whatever else you *do*. We all know that children are a gift from God. I did not properly receive or open those gifts. The two greatest gifts God gave me were Shannon and Shawn, but I missed out on some special times because I was so driven with my work.

Drive, passion, and a strong work ethic are admirable traits, but they must be balanced with family, or, if you don't have family, then with those you love and those who love you. I'm convinced by now that nothing is more important in this life than relationships.

All those years, I thought I had found my purpose through baseball, but I was so wrong. Much of my purpose was right before my eyes in my family, whom I sadly tended to neglect. And before I knew it, baseball would be stripped away. I would make it to the top of Major League Baseball and realize that I didn't like the view.

Errors and Idols

There's an interesting moment in Exodus when Moses's father-in-law notices how Moses is unhealthily consumed in his work and task before him. "What you are doing is not very good," his father-in-law confronts Moses. "The work is too heavy for you; you cannot handle it alone."

We all have idols that get in the way of our call. An idol in the Old Testament was a false god that took the place of the one true, living God. In our culture, we might erect idols when we place our careers over God or chase success over our families. These idols cloud our spiritual vision and distract us from our true call: to love God and others.

Part of scouting the enemy is realizing our own cultural idols—work, production, money, wealth, fame, etc.—and our tendencies to pursue what culture elevates. Again, we ask ourselves if we are citizens of the world or citizens of heaven. If we are citizens of the world, we will pursue what the world deems important. If we awaken more to our true citizenship in heaven, we will pursue what God elevates: love, compassion, service, justice, etc.

Acknowledging our idols forces us to consider what *true* purpose is all about. In Genesis 11:1-9 we read about a group of nomadic people who settle on a plain in Shinar (which is Babylonia). It didn't take long for them to become engrossed in building a city, which included a tower that stretched into the sky. "Come, let us build ourselves a city," we're told the people say in Genesis 11:4, "with a tower that reaches to the heavens, so that we may make a name for ourselves; otherwise we will be scattered over the face of the whole earth."

Let's not forget that these people *felt* they were doing something meaningful. Yet, their claim is telling. "Let's make a name for ourselves," they said. They may as well have been describing the American mindset thousands of years before such a thing existed.

I'm sure you've probably heard it said that EGO stands for *edging God out*. How many people are caught up in a relentless chase for that which feeds their ego instead of partnering with God to bring His love into the world? Or, perhaps the motive is more subtle. For example, I may not have been interested in seeing my name in shining lights, but there is no doubt that I was completely tunnel-visioned chasing championships. This came at the expense of missing my kids' birthdays, school projects, athletics contests, and many other family events.

I've always had that chip on my shoulder, and too often that ambition has called the shots, even subconsciously. Maybe it goes back to my dad's frequent disapproval of me. Or to the priest's abuse. I don't know. I've come to learn, however, that insecurity is still ego.

Pursuing world championships while staying anchored in God is possible, but there was a desperation to my chase. You could say I was out to prove I was worthy rather than trusting in my inherent worthiness in Christ. I justified the tower I was building because of the opportunities my success attracted. As I became more successful and well-known, I was invited to speak at Christian breakfasts, to be interviewed by Christian publications about my faith. It's not that I was a hypocrite. I remember praying with several players going through a tough time, once in the hotel room of an "all-star" who was in the middle of a personal crisis—I doubt many General Managers were doing things like that. I tried to let my faith guide me at work, but the problem was that work was life when it should have been third in my priorities: faith, family, baseball.

And, before I knew it, that tower I had been building at the expense of valuable time with my family would come crashing down.

8

IMPLOSION

"God is using your present circumstances to make you more useful
for later roles in His unfolding story."
~Louis Giglio

When I took the General Manager position with the Los
Angeles Dodgers in August 1998, the media world was
in the midst of several transitions. The twenty-four-hour news
cycle was proving to be profitable as cable networks began transitioning toward more inflammatory and one-sided news. Newspapers were also beginning to gain more revenue via Internet advertising, thus the need to drive clicks through baiting you with a
headline. That would only worsen in the next two decades with
the rise of social media. But those were the beginning stages of a
new era of sensationalist journalism.

All of these transitions conflated in Los Angeles. The year the
Dodgers hired me, the team made some organizational shifts.
After fifty-two years of ownership by the O'Malley family, Rupert
Murdoch's Fox Entertainment Group acquired the Dodgers. I
was excited to help the Dodgers build a championship team, but
I became associated with a new regime of corporate ownership.
FOX was becoming a serious power player in cable news, and

several other news outlets feared their thriving model.

I quickly discovered the difference between the scope of Los Angeles media and the other places I had worked. I had always dealt straight with the media, but I learned the hard way that in LA, I had to be ultra-careful about my words.

When I jokingly told them there was a new sheriff in town, I unknowingly gave some media the ammo they needed to paint me as a cocky destroyer of tradition. When I was asked what my nickname was, I shrugged and said, "You can call me 'Dodger Boy.'" You would have thought by the reaction that I was equating myself with legends like Sandy Koufax and Tommy Lasorda. Anything I gave the media that was even remotely edgy could be twisted to form a particular narrative: this new regime was looking to dismantle Dodger tradition!

Nonetheless, I started making moves, as I had been hired to do. After signing pitcher Kevin Brown to the first nine-figure contract in the MLB, making several trades (because we were so right-handed hitting dominant in our lineup as a team), and watching manager Mike Scioscia (who I encouraged to lead our Triple-A affiliate to get some managing experience) get signed by the Anaheim Angels one year later and eventually lead them to a World Series, well, the media had their narrative. I was a jester who confused himself for a white knight. You would have thought by their coverage that I was the dumbest person in baseball.

If I could go back and do it again, I would make pretty much all the same personnel moves I made. I *would* change how open and accessible I was to the media. I would have been more guarded. I tend to say some unpolished things—to say exactly what I think.

For two years, I saw writers' stories become less objective and more inflammatory. They never attacked my character—but fueled the narrative that I was incompetent. Progress had indeed been slower than I had hoped, but it's not like I had come in and dismantled a championship team, which you would have thought I had done by the narrative that the media spun. The Dodgers hadn't won a playoff game in ten years, since their World Series title in 1988.

In my first year, 1999, we finished 77-85 and third in our division. In my second year, 2000, we improved to 86-76 and barely missed the playoffs. We were on the up-and-up, albeit slower than I hoped. Our farm system was improving. Management must've felt I was doing a good job with our reconstruction because they gave me a sizable bonus after my second year. I felt good about the pieces we had in place but was dissatisfied with the media turmoil that seemed to swirl around our team perpetually.

So often throughout my second year, Tommy Lasorda would come bursting into my office with a newspaper clipping and a peeved look.

"Did you see what the media said?" he'd ask me, pointing to a quote that often was from me.

"That's not what I said, Tommy," I told him often. "Here's what I really said…"

The stories made me seem like I had a notorious way of "putting my foot in my mouth," as my boss Bob Daly would later say about me. But it also always felt that my quotes were taken out of context and dramatized.

Mentally, I was not in a good place that year. For the first time, I began to adopt something of a victim mentality. Once I began to believe the media was out to get me, I began to think *everyone* was out to get me. I felt misunderstood by the media and now felt as though *everyone* misunderstood me, even those I loved and who loved me, like my family. I inappropriately handled the pressure and stress. At home, Marilyn and I weren't seeing eye-to-eye. In retrospect, I can see that I was taking my frustration and disappointment out on her. I felt isolated. I had a three-week phase where I hardly ate and wanted to stay in bed. I was spiraling into a black hole, and even getting up and showering was challenging. It hit me that I wasn't in control. Depression to any degree can be debilitating. It definitely was for me.

In the context of everything discussed in the last chapter,

perhaps you can see how the tower I had built was beginning to crack. If I was working sixteen to twenty hours a day (and I was) and *still* couldn't control something as simple as a media narrative, what was I to do? I was working harder than ever before, living in my office, sometimes sleeping on the floor, but the harder I worked, the more the media's narrative continued to spiral.

The chip on my shoulder I had always carried with me got bigger. My desperation for success deepened. My tunnel-vision somehow narrowed more. I was *determined* to prove everyone wrong. The only way to be happy again, I wrongly believed, was to win.

I normally like a good challenge. In Montreal, I loved the challenge of building a team despite having what felt like a minor league budget. In Baltimore, I loved the challenge of working alongside Hall of Fame Pat Gillick and trying to get an iconic franchise back to the playoffs for the first time since they won a World Series in 1983. We did. The Orioles made it to the ALCS in both 1996 and 1997. When I came to Los Angeles, I was invigorated for many of the same reasons: the challenge of bringing a historic franchise back to prominence and creating a culture that aligned with their rich tradition—but two straight years of a relentless media storm had flung me into an unfamiliar mental and emotional space that I didn't know how to navigate.

I felt there was no reprieve.

I was in a fight for my professional baseball life.

All I wanted to do was focus all my energy on building a championship team, but I made it a goal of mine during spring training of my third season to try to smooth out things with the media. Maybe there was something I could be doing better to help *them*. Perhaps they had a fundamental misunderstanding about *me*.

One evening, I took all media members out to dinner. I encouraged them to call me on my cell phone if they needed anything. I told them that I wanted to help them do their jobs the best they could and provide them with helpful information as the season unfolded. I had been accessible to them already, but I wanted to be completely accessible and reemphasize that I valued transparency.

I also asked them over dinner that night to give me a legitimate chance. I hadn't been the most pragmatic general manager in MLB. I was enthusiastic and loud. I preferred to provide honest and sometimes blunt answers to questions instead of public relations balderdash. I needed them to see through my rhetoric and paint the bigger picture, if indeed that picture was the truth. After all, their job as journalists was to communicate what was *really* happening, not twist the truth to fit their narrative. Of course, I didn't expect them to write all positive stories about me or the Dodgers. After two straight years of missing the playoffs, I deserved criticism and scrutiny. But it was also true that we were getting better, that the pieces were falling into place, and that management must have felt good about the job I was doing.

Then came another tidal wave.

Avalanche

During 2001 spring training, our owner, Bob Daly, got into a pissing match with one of our stars, Gary Sheffield. Both are great guys, but they also had massive egos. I couldn't get them on the same page regarding Gary's contract. The lack of resolution and the looming reality that one of the Dodgers' best stars might not return caused another media spiral. It again came back to me. They began putting pressure on Bob, relentlessly questioning him whether I was the right guy for the job. I went into survival, fighting mode.

I knew keeping Gary was best for both our team and the fans. But, since teams around the league knew that Bob wanted Gary traded, I received laughable deals from other General Managers. They knew they had all the leverage and that I was stuck between a rock and a hard place. After feeling I had explored all my options, I tore off my proverbial gloves. I told Bob, "If you want to trade him, then *you* trade him. I'm not doing it!"

I knew a trade wasn't best for the team and the fans.

The situation aligned perfectly with the media's two-year narrative that I was unfit for the job. Even though the final decision was not mine.

Around this time, I got a call from the Assistant Chief of Police in charge of communications at the Los Angeles Police Department. He asked me to come by the academy, which was right next to Dodger Stadium, because he wanted to talk to me about something. Mystified by the invitation, I swung by.

"You're going to get fired," he told me bluntly.

"What do you mean?" I asked.

He explained there is a strategic method for when the Los Angeles media come after police chiefs. He pointed out the strategic placement of different stories throughout the newspaper, all feeding into the same narrative. To this day, I have no idea if any of this is true or if this media "strategy" was as intentional as he theorized, but it certainly aligned with my experience. The media turmoil was an unstoppable avalanche.

I tried to fight the darkness, but the pressure was unbearable. For over two years, I felt I was falling infinitely into a black hole. I know something of what gymnast Simone Biles said she felt in the 2021 Olympics when she stepped away from competition because of concerns about her mental health. While I was not in the same physical danger as she would have been when attempting unfathomable flips and twirls in midair as a gymnast, I could relate to the extreme pressure and a deep knowing that I was not in the right headspace.

In the following months, the Assistant Chief of Police's prediction seemed to be coming true. I would think I had a good conversation with a member of the media, but then I would read their story and think to myself, *What in the world?* I grew even more angry. Whatever I did, whatever I didn't do, I was always guilty in the media's eyes. I once called a prominent writer who knowingly twisted my words after an interview to formulate an eye-catching headline. "You know none of this is true," I confronted him.

His response? "GM, the truth doesn't matter."

I knew then that the writing was on the wall. A narrative had been established that was driving media traffic. There was no going back. This was "cancel culture" before that term existed. I had to fight my anger and remember my mission field—that these writers had families to care for and likely faced pressures from their editors in the ever-shifting media landscape, and newspapers were quickly being left behind.

I began to hear grumblings in media circles that Bob was looking for my replacement despite having just given me a bonus. One day, he called me, and I ignored his call. He was my boss, and I was supposed to call him right back. I didn't.

When the Dodgers traveled to San Diego—the city I was born in when my dad was stationed in the Navy—to take on the Padres early that season, we were in first place. Marilyn, Shannon, and Shawn attended the games with me on Friday and Saturday, then returned to Los Angeles to celebrate Shannon's birthday with her friends. Shawn and I stayed for the game on Sunday. He loved going into the clubhouse, loading up on candy and soda, and being on the field with the players during batting practice.

During the game, a fan in front of me began yelling inflammatory things at Gary Sheffield. "You're an embarrassment, Sheffield!" he screamed repeatedly. Recognizing me, he began chirping at me as well, right in front of Shawn. When Gary hit a two-run home run that maybe made it ten feet off the ground, I turned toward him, pointed at his team, and said, "Now *that's* an embarrassment."

Later in the game, he continued running his mouth. "Dodger Boy, how about you go get an interview with another team?"

The guy obviously knew his stuff and was aware that my head was on the chopping block. Weirdly enough, I saw piñatas of my face at San Diego's stadium that weekend, which I actually thought was kind of cool.

After the fan commented about me finding another job, I said, "Come up here, and I'll give you an interview."

Our exchange that game was less heated and more comical and

entertaining to the fans around us. He annoyed me, but I'm sure I annoyed him too. It was fun sports banter. Little did I know that this man was a part-time writer in San Diego.

Shawn and I left after the sixth inning, and by the time I got home, I received a frantic call from the Dodgers Public Relations Director. "Did you beat up a fan in San Diego?" he exclaimed. "It's being reported that you got in a fight."

"What?" I said. "No, I was with my son, and we left in the sixth inning to drive back to Los Angeles."

Someone told the *Los Angeles Times* I had gotten in a fight at the game. The next day, Bob summoned me for a meeting at his home. Holding up a copy of the *Times*, he screamed, "You're a f*&%ing lightning rod!"

I think we were all sick of the media charade, desperate for some kind of reprieve. To his credit, with the target I had on my back, it was foolish of me—the General Manager of the Dodgers—to even entertain the idea of engaging with a fan. The story the *Times* reported couldn't have been further from the truth, but I was silly to exchange words with someone considering my position with the team.

"I have no choice but to fire you," Bob told me that day.

"Bob," I pleaded, "it's not true. You know me. You know I've always put the team first. And would I really do what the *Times* accuses me of in front of my son?"

It didn't matter. Bob felt backed into a corner by the media, as did I.

We've all seen this dynamic on display, haven't we? What happened to me in Los Angeles was a microcosm of how media intensity can distort the truth. Some felt a sense of self-righteousness or a larger-than-life purpose to get me fired. We often see this same self-righteousness and religious zeal displayed in people's social justice fights, even at the expense of the truth.

We ought to be aware of how canceling, shaming, and scapegoating get confused for justice. As much as I might disagree with most of former president Barack Obama's politics, he was correct when he called out young activists at the 2019 Obama Foundation Summit. His profound words are worth including in full: "I do get a sense sometimes now among certain young people, and this is accelerated by social media, there is this sense sometimes of: 'The way of me making change is to be as judgmental as possible about other people,' and that's enough. Like, if I tweet or hashtag about how you didn't do something right or used the wrong verb, then I can sit back and feel pretty good about myself, 'cause, 'Man, you see how woke I was, I called you out.' That's not activism. That's not bringing about change. If all you're doing is casting stones, you're probably not going to get that far. That's easy to do."

Maybe I *still* wouldn't have turned the Dodgers around even had I been given a couple more years, but I'm convinced that my departure from the Dodgers—after less than three years of working for them—was the direct result of a biased media that invested in a fabricated narrative over the truth of the situation.

Feeling backed into a corner and that my character had been attacked, I would later hire a private investigator to uncover the details from that afternoon in San Diego. In their interviews, all the fans around us said the same thing: that we were just occasionally jawing with one another and that it was playful and entertaining. Every camera revealed there was no such thing as a fight. I just wanted the truth out there, but this move, too, apparently proved my paranoia and desperation. I was on the gallows, and there was no taking me back down.

I had no idea that God was waking me up.

The Burning Bush

The good thing about my experience in Los Angeles is that, disgusted with baseball and media, I had space to consider a different kind of life. My brokenness led me back to my family, to making God the center of my life, to serving, and to ministry.

During my seven years in a General Manager position, I would sometimes share my testimony at men's breakfasts or try to use my influence to help people. Still, service was more of an afterthought, not something at the forefront of my life. In Los Angeles, God tried to wake me from my selfishness when I was exposed to the incredible work that Pastor Matthew Barnett and the Los Angeles Dream Center were doing as they fought injustice in the epicenter of America. But anytime my heart was stirred to get more involved, I always allowed myself to get more caught up in the professional demands of my job.

I had championships to win. Until one day, I didn't.

In Exodus 3 is one of the greatest moments in all of Scripture. Moses seemed to be settled into his new life in Midian. He was no longer a foreigner in a foreign land. He was married to the daughter of a Midian priest. He and Zipporah had a child, Gershom. At the end of Exodus 2 we read that a "long period" passed in which the king of Egypt died, and the Israelites became more restless in their state of enslavement. As I've mentioned, some scholars believe it had been at least forty years since Moses fled Egypt.

We can almost picture Moses having a certain kind of contentment with his new life. Pharaoh, the man who sought to have Moses killed upon hearing about the killing of the Egyptian guard, was long gone. Scripture is unclear whether Moses had become reacquainted with his Hebrew roots or if Midian was simply a safe haven from Pharaoh's wrath and the grip of slavery on the Israelites. It was likely the latter. Zipporah was not an Israelite. Nonetheless, Moses was safe, content, and belonged to a priest's family who had some sense of local status. But then everything changed.

In Exodus 3, we read that Moses was going about his daily duties, tending the flock of his father-in-law. And that was when God came rushing into Moses's mundane world.

God spoke to Moses through a burning bush that miraculously did not burn down. Exodus 3:4 says, "When the Lord saw that he had gone over to look, God called to him from within the bush, 'Moses! Moses!'"

God can come bursting into our lives in the most unexpected times. God came to Moses amidst his routines, chores, and through a humble, unassuming bush. When Moses least expected it, God revealed Himself and asked Moses to listen.

We all have burning bush moments—when God meets us where we are and screams for our attention; those times when our world shatters, and we have no one else to depend on but God; those times when the glow of a burning bush blinds us. I've learned that *we* have to open ourselves up to the possibility that God is in our midst—even when He is the last thing we want to think about. Perhaps *especially* when we don't want to think about Him.

I may not have realized it then, but getting fired from the Dodgers was my burning bush moment. I had become content with a life absorbed in baseball, yet my priorities were out of whack. When my career came crashing down—the career I had worked so hard to build at the expense of my family—I was suddenly left to contend with what life was really about.

God got Moses's full attention. Without a doubt, God got my attention. As my baseball career fell apart, God placed a Bible verse on my heart, Job 1:21, that touched me greatly: "Naked I came from my mother's womb, and naked I will depart. The Lord gave, and the Lord has taken away; may the name of the Lord be praised." That verse has become a part of who I am—I *do* try to praise Him every day.

There's no doubt I could have stayed in baseball. Just a few years before, I was named General Manager of the Year. After the Dodgers debacle, I likely would have had to take the GM position at a small-market team or an Assistant GM position at a larger team, but why would I? I had made it to the top of the mountain and didn't like the view. Why would I try to climb the mountain again?

My question for you is this: Could God be trying to get your attention when your idols crumble, when you feel the emptiness of getting everything you ever wanted? Could God have a bigger purpose for you beyond your sense of safety and contentment? Could your world be lighting up with God's presence when you least expect it?

Most people spend their lives going through the motions. They work hard, gain wealth, retire, and then ride off into the sunset. Most men my age are retired by now, but I feel that I'm in the biggest fight of my life. Everything I experienced as a General Manager in baseball, and all that we went through as a family, have propelled me into the crux of my purpose: to fight human trafficking.

9
RECONSTRUCT

"All that is necessary for the triumph of evil is for good men to do nothing."
~Edmund Burke

The Dodgers implosion sent me on a journey. Instead of immediately seeking a new job in baseball, I decided to take some time. The Dodgers paid me a substantial amount to stay home (one and a half years of salary), and I embarked on a spiritual search detached from baseball. It didn't take too long for me to realize that getting fired was a blessing.

Shannon was a talented softball player, and I was able to coach her throughout her high school career and have a front-row seat to her receiving All-League honors in her junior and senior years. As Shawn made his way through junior high, I was able to coach him in basketball. I *loved* being a more involved and present father and husband. It also came with a bit of a sting as I realized what I had been missing out on all those years. Family meals. Movie nights. School functions. Athletic events. I felt like God was giving me a second chance at fatherhood.

It was tough when Shawn got sucked into the wrong crowd in

high school and began experimenting with partying and drugs. He was a brilliant kid, the salutatorian of his class. Watching him flirt with throwing all that down the drain was painful, but at least Marilyn did not have to navigate that alone, as she probably would have had I still been working in baseball. Being a father is a tremendous gift. Our children should be a priority. I had to learn this the hard way, but I'm thankful I finally came around. I learned the importance of being a father before it was too late. It's a fantastic privilege and a true blessing to be a dad.

For years, throughout Shawn's spiral into addiction, Marilyn and I cried together and prayed together. When Shawn overdosed (chapter one of this book), we *fought* for Shawn together when doctors suggested that we pull his feeding tube, and when he miraculously emerged from his coma, we nursed him back to health—*together*. He could not remember how to eat, walk, or even talk. He had to re-learn how to formulate sentences. He was so dependent on us that I felt God was saying to me, "Kevin, now you have a chance to be the father you never were."

Each new day I got with my son flooded my heart with gratitude. "I gave you your son back," I felt that God told me, "Now I want you to help give other children back to their families." Seeds were being planted in my fighting heart to become an anti-human-trafficking activist.

That was one of the big mental breakthroughs in my own life. When Shawn miraculously came out of his dark coma, I realized there were so many other children in our own country yet to come out of the darkness of human trafficking.

We were able to advocate for Shawn in the hospital. We could invest in his healing as he showed us new signs of hope. But who was advocating for young boys and girls raped several times a day, manipulated by a parent-like figure into having survival sex for money, and whose unfathomable darkness, like the enslaved Hebrew people, had become the only life they knew?

Falling Upward

I had experimented with many things to support my family finan-cially during those post-baseball years, but every road led back to activism. I became good friends with pastor and theologian John MacArthur and fundraised for his Bible College. I co-owned a Mercedes-Benz auto dealership. I fundraised full-time for the Los Angeles Dream Center. Opportunities arose to get back into baseball, but I resisted. I liked being a family man. I liked the consistency and predictability in my schedule, which gave me the flexibility to get more involved in my local church and other charitable organizations and, for the first time, have time to go on mission trips. I credit those trips to Israel, Thailand, and Uganda with expanding my perspective and reminding me that life—that *purpose*—is about selfless service.

In 2006 my family took an amazing trip along with Wayne McCall and his family to Uganda, Africa. I was blessed to have been there a few years before with a small group of pastors, including Francis Chan. We went to train and teach hundreds of Ugandan pastors the Bible, as well as visit some IDP (Inter-nally Displaced People) camps in Northern Uganda. We visited refugee camps in Siroti, Lira, and Gulu to see how we could best help them.

When our two families landed at Entebbe Airport in Kampala, Uganda, we met up with Peter Habyirmana, a young man from Uganda who I had met while he was a student at The Master's University in northern Los Angeles. Marilyn and I considered Peter our (unofficial) adopted son, as we did our best to take care of him for several years. On our trip, we served poor villages by providing various supplies, food, and money. We took signifi-cant resources with us in order to be a blessing to the people of Uganda. After a few days in the Kampala area, we traveled north to a town called Siroti, stopping at small villages along the way. At each location we had the privilege to spend quality time with these beautiful people and in most cases even worship with them. Worshiping with Africans is special, as they are truly in love with

Jesus and enthusiastic in song and dance. It's a full and whole-hearted experience.

Next we ventured to Gulu, another IDP camp with tens of thousands of people living there. These refugees had fled the warlord Joseph Kony, a leader of the Lord's Resistance Army who was known for burning down villages, killing adults, turning girls into sex slaves, and the boys into soldiers. After ten days of traveling the dusty roads of Uganda, spending blessed time with thousands of people, both families headed home to the United States. I stayed another two weeks. I felt called further. God was already stirring my heart for justice: to fight for the vulnerable and serve those who were suffering.

In the mid-2000s, my family and I started attending Cornerstone Church in Simi Valley, California. I became good friends with the head pastor, Francis Chan. God was working on his heart about human trafficking at the same time He was working on mine. Francis was connected to the Children's Hunger Fund, and I was connected to Zoe International. These organizations partnered together. In 2009, Francis and I went on a trip to Thailand with a group of men.

The trip crushed me. We visited the slums of Mae Sot and witnessed first-hand the horrors of severe poverty. It felt like we were on another planet or back in a primitive time. In Chiang Mai, we visited a safe home for fifty or sixty kids who had been trafficked. I saw little four, five, and six-year-olds who had been sex slaves.

Many nights during that trip, I returned to the hotel room I shared with Francis, overwhelmed with the day's heaviness. Francis, a consummate pastor, would listen patiently to me as I processed what I had seen and heard that day. He felt no need to offer advice or conjure some theological explanation for the darkness we were encountering. He simply listened. Had it not been so dark in our hotel room, I wonder if he would have been able to see my heart breaking in front of him. I wonder if he could also see that, at a time in my fifties when most men were settling into their lives and beginning to think about retirement, I was still filled with dreams and an aching desire to *do something* about what I had seen.

When I returned to the States, I obsessively began digging for more information. What I thought was more of an international problem turned out to be just as much of an issue in the United States. We're pretty good at that in America, aren't we? Thinking we can solve other country's problems while epidemics on our own soil go unaddressed? It's an extremely unfortunate misconception that trafficking isn't a problem in America.

Did you know that human trafficking generates $9.5 billion a year in the United States? The U.S. Department of Justice estimates that 300,000 children are at risk of being sex trafficked, with an average age of thirteen to fourteen. The typical victim may be forced to have sex up to ten to fifteen, possibly twenty times a day, as the Polaris Project has reported. A trafficker approaches homeless and runaways within forty-eight hours of being on the street.

I had long been praying, "God, break my heart for what breaks Yours." Nothing had ever broken my heart quite like looking into the eyes of those children who had their childhoods ripped away.

I had always been a fighter. I had always been passionate and fiery. I felt God was telling me to engage, fight, and redefine what winning championships meant. He wanted me to be genuinely purposeful with my energy, time, and resources—and to enter the human trafficking fight.

I remember, after I had moved on from baseball, a media member hearing about how I was engaged in a different business, fundraising endeavors, and various Christian missions. Surprised that I hadn't tried to get back into baseball, he said to me, "Dang, Kevin, you've really fallen off the map, haven't you?"

I laughed and told him, "No, I've fallen upward."

Active Justice

As Moses questions the burning bush in Exodus 3 and learns

that this is the great "I Am," Yahweh, the God of the Israelites, the Lord's response is one that I invite you to meditate upon. For emphasis, I've italicized the verbs the Lord is said to have told Moses.

"I have indeed *seen* the misery of my people in Egypt. I have *heard* them crying out because of their slave drivers, and I am *concerned* about their suffering. So I have *come* down to *rescue* them from the hand of the Egyptians and to *bring* them up out of that land into a good and spacious land flowing with milk and honey. And now the cry of the Israelites has reached me, and I have *seen* the way the Egyptians are oppressing them. So now, go. I am *sending* you to Pharaoh to bring my people, the Israelites, out of Egypt."

Notice in the passage how active God becomes in the Israelites' suffering. He *sees* their misery. He *hears* their cries. Not only does Yahweh see and hear the pain of the Israelites, but He also notices how the Egyptians are oppressing the Israelites. In other words, Yahweh has a genuine concern for both the victim and the oppressor and becomes determined to do something about it—*through* Moses.

I've found over time that God's call to justice is one of the purest calls of all. In this passage of Scripture, we, too, encounter a God who cares deeply about His people, a God who hears the cries of the enslaved, a God who is seriously concerned about suffering, a God determined to come down and rescue the mistreated. We are each invited to follow the same trajectory as Moses: to partner with God as our hearts break for what breaks God's heart—to help liberate the abused in this broken world.

Whatever issue (or issues) of injustice God has placed on your heart probably has something to do with human dignity. If it doesn't, I'd argue that the calling probably isn't coming from God.

Is there a call that you've felt in your own life? What are the spiritual dimensions of that call? I've learned that the spiritual dimensions of a call always have something to do with helping others.

A call from God, in my opinion, is always about the kingdom of God. When called, your ability, skills, talents, and experiences are to be used for God. As Tim Keller says, "God's call humbles, breaks, disturbs, convicts, and shakes us."

God's call is radical, and its purpose is to bless others.

The call of God to me—and I'd argue, on some level, for all of us—is to surrender, die to selfishness, and make life less about us and more about Him. Jesus was to increase, and we are to decrease. With this lifestyle of surrender comes true fulfillment and satisfaction.

When God called me to a new fight, and I left behind a sport that had been such a big part of my life, I felt as though I was going through an emptying process— as if God was penetrating my existence or trying to get my attention. I could sense His loving presence. As love does, it was sending me forth.

It's scary to let our idols crumble, to trust God's call completely. Considering a new way of life and moving beyond what is comfortable is disorienting. But let's cling to God's words to Moses in Exodus 3:12: "*I will be with you.*" Meditate upon those five words as you contemplate your call. The God of justice promises to be with us every step of the way. Jesus famously echoed this in what is known as the "Great Commission" in Matthew 28 when he says, "Therefore go and make disciples of all nations, baptizing them in the name of the Father and of the Son and of the Holy Spirit, and teaching them to obey everything I have commanded you. And surely I am with you always, to the very end of the age."

If you remember anything from this book, I hope it's these three words, spoken by Yahweh to Moses, "So now, *go.*"

PART II
JUSTICE

10
WHO AM I?

"Christians today like to play it safe. We want to put ourselves in situations where we are safe 'even if there is no God.' But if we truly desire to please God, we cannot live that way."
~Francis Chan

To go is to trust—that we are loved, chosen, and predestined to do great things for God's kingdom. Few understand this spiritual truth better than the Jewish people.

Following my departure from the Dodgers, I became involved with several Jewish organizations. This journey into Judaism began when I went to Israel for the first time in 2005 with Dr. Will Varner, a Bible professor at The Master's University in Los Angeles. I have gone a total of eight times. Soon, I hope to be making my ninth trip to Israel.

To say it was love at first sight during that first visit would be quite an understatement. In the Holy Land, I felt, in some unique way, the genuine presence of God. That first visit was also special because my daughter Shannon (a student at The Master's University) was with me. I didn't sleep for two or three nights on the trip. I was on spiritual overload.

Seeing the biblical sites that I had been reading about in my

Bible since I had that life-changing encounter with Jesus Christ in 1979 was an unforgettable experience. The Word of God that I had been reading in black and white came alive with color as I saw the locations of biblical history. My visits to Israel have helped me fall even more in love with Scripture, which I believe is the authoritative and inerrant Word of God. I can't get enough of the Word and am confident it is the best way to get to know God.

My pilgrimages to Israel have especially helped bring to life the Old Testament, which often feels odd or obscure to our modern ears. Also known as the Jewish Tanakh, the Old Testament begins with the Torah (the first five books), which includes the creation story, the history of the patriarchs, and the exodus from Egypt— the main thread of this book, which to me encapsulates the universal search for purpose and call to justice. The Jewish Tanakh also includes the Prophet and Wisdom books, which have numerous prophecies about the Messiah, Jesus. The New Testament reveals the coming of Jesus—His birth, life, death, and resurrection, His teachings, and those of His disciples.

Israel helped me fall more in love with God's Word, which has helped me grow in my knowledge of Israel and the importance of the Holy Land. Simply put, I love Israel because God loves Israel. God *chose* Israel, as we read in Deuteronomy 7:6: "For you are a people holy to the Lord your God. The Lord your God has chosen you to be a people for His treasured possession, out of all the peoples on the face of the earth." I realize that Israel is not perfect and far from it, but I think it's important to know that God wants us to honor and bless Israel. As we read in Genesis 12:3, "I will bless those who bless you (Israel), and him who dishonors you I will curse, and in you all the families of the earth shall be blessed."

God's promises for Israel still stand today. Replacement theology, the belief that American Christians have replaced Jews as God's chosen people, is egocentric and wrong. Ironically, the people who adopt this toxic theology struggle to see those different from them as "chosen." They struggle to let their faith guide them outward to help heal the hurting people of this world, to see how inherently connected they are to those they might disagree with. Jesus's two greatest commandments in Matthew 22:36-40 are to "Love the Lord your God with all your heart and with all your soul and with all your mind" and to "Love your neighbor as yourself." Jesus says nothing about your neighbor having to be someone who believes the same things as you. As Christians, we ought to strive to see those who are suffering as our dearest neighbors.

Christians have not replaced Jews as God's Chosen People, and the church has not replaced God's purpose, plan, and promises. I believe Israel is not an aggressor state but is highly defensive and protecting its existence. The Bible is clear that Israel is the spiritual root of Christianity's hope and faith in the God of Israel. Christians seem to forget Jesus was a Jew.

People consider me a Christian Zionist because I am committed to being involved through prayer and practical support in what God is doing in the world through Israel. Christian Zionism is based on the Word of God for the sake of Israel and the Jewish people. One of the Jewish organizations in which I serve as a "Friendraiser" is called World Emunah Israel. *Emunah* is a Hebrew word for faith. As Hebrews 11:1 says, "Now faith is confidence in what we hope for and assurance about what we do not see." Faith engages life's complexities, sufferings, and horrors—these avenues we cannot see—and chooses hope amid the darkness. That's what World Emunah does. They come alongside some of the most vulnerable children in Israel, whose lives are often tattered by war and violence, by neglect, and break the cycle of distress. They have children's homes, high schools, daycare centers, counseling and crisis centers. Two other organizations I love, support, and help are Hope for Israel and Hayovel.

One of the many things I admire about Judaism is their faith and trust in their own "chosenness," the belief that God has hand-picked them to do great things. Not great things based on selfish, worldly reasons, but because God would get the glory from these things they are called to do. I'm undoubtedly a human trafficking activist because of the parallels I see between these forgotten children and the Jewish people throughout history.

Remembering One's Chosenness

Let's not forget that the challenges for the Jews did not end after their four hundred and fifty years of enslavement by the Egyptians. They spent the next forty years in exile before settling in the Promised Land and making Jerusalem their capital around 1000 B.C.

In 586 B.C., after four centuries in their Promised Land, the Babylonians sieged Jerusalem and cut the Jewish people off from their surrounding farmland. Corpses piled up. Starvation was rampant. As it says in Lamentations 4:4, "The tongue of the suckling child cleaves to the roof of his mouth for thirst. The young children ask for bread, and no one breaks it for them."

Today, children who are being trafficked cry out for this same nourishment. Will we break bread for them?

The Babylonians would eventually breach the city and slaughter the Jewish people. Not long after the invasion, the Babylonian armies set Jerusalem ablaze, including the Jewish temple, which remains a day of mourning for the Jewish people called the 9th of Av.

All this may have happened in the Old Testament, but as we all know, this persecution of the Jewish people has continued into the twentieth and twenty-first centuries. Their faith has been tested in ways that are beyond comprehension. It wasn't that long ago that six *million* Jews were executed by Nazis in Germany who believed the Arian race to be "racially superior" to the "inferior" Jews. It's sobering to remember that this was only two to three generations ago and that America mostly sat on the sidelines of the war until *we* were attacked at Pearl Harbor.

Prior to this book going to print Israel suffered a massacre on the Jewish holiday Simchat Torah by the terrorist organization Hamas, whose charter calls for the destruction of Israel and death of all Jews through Jihad. Over 1,400 Israeli civilians and thirty Americans were killed. More than 4,000 were injured, and 200 babies, children, women, and elderly were taken as hostages. Israel, seeking to defend itself, declared war against Hamas on October 7, 2023. I was scheduled to be in Israel later that month, but that trip was postponed. I am dedicated to personally donating and raising money to help Israel protect its citizens and provide relief for the victims of this terrorist attack. No scouting the enemy needed on this evil, it's time to take action.

Amidst today's radicalism and division, anti-Semitic attacks have risen in America. In January 2022, four hostages were taken at a synagogue in Texas. In October 2018, eleven people were killed at a Pittsburgh synagogue. In April 2014 a neo-Nazi and Klansman killed three at a Jewish retirement community in Kansas. In July 2006, a violent Muslim extremist shot six women, one fatally, at the Jewish Federation of Greater Seattle. The Anti-Defamation League (ADL) found that antisemitic incidents increased in the U.S. by thirty-five percent between 2021 and 2022. Anti-semitic hate crimes rose in New York, Los Angeles, and Chicago, where the country's largest Jewish populations reside.

I wonder if one of the many reasons the Jewish people have been able to persevere through it all—despite discrimination and being targets of genocide—is because of their unshakable belief that God has chosen them to do great things. That doesn't mean that no one else is chosen. Anti-semites want you to think Jews are exclusive and arrogant. Chosenness is an *empowering* claim, which faith is supposed to be at its core. I might disagree with the Jewish interpretation of Jesus, but when you start to see the "other" as "God's chosen people," you'll begin to see that God wants *everyone* to be His chosen people.

As God called me more deeply into the human trafficking fight, I couldn't help but lean on the core Jewish wisdom I had absorbed over the years.

I needed that wisdom because I couldn't help but sometimes

doubt my path into activism. Who was *I* to enter such a war? Yes, human trafficking is a war, a physical and spiritual war. What could *I* possibly do about such a massive problem? Could God use someone like *me*, this person who had made so many mistakes throughout my life—from my rowdy college days to my workaholism in Major League Baseball, to my inability to bite my tongue as the GM of the Dodgers—to fight modern-day slavery? I had no experience in social justice. I had never started a nonprofit. I had never led a ministry—I had never finished seminary! My expertise was in baseball—and *now* I was going to fight child sex trafficking?

At times, my life path seemed so baffling.

But then I would think of the theological idea of chosenness. I'd think of Shannon. And Shawn. I would think of God's tug on my heart after He miraculously brought Shawn back to life, back into my and Marilyn's loving arms. I had no idea where to start when it came to fighting child sex trafficking, an epidemic that unfolds in the shadows in every American zip code, each of which has reported at least one sex trafficking case in their community. All I knew was this: I left my heart in Thailand.

Christians believe in this chosenness too but, for some reason, are more inclined to adopt a negative, victim mentality. Maybe that's because some of their theology is more rooted in human-kind's fallenness and brokenness than God's love and grace. As Paul writes in Ephesians 2:10, "For we are God's handiwork, created in Christ Jesus to do good works, which God prepared in advance for us to do."

Our journeys toward justice—toward a liberation-centered purpose—require genuinely believing and trusting that we are chosen. Not to lift ourselves up or attain worldly things, but to help and heal the world.

Acknowledging and confronting the horrific situations the youth of our world are navigating is truly difficult and disorient-ing. That's one reason many simply turn a comfortable blind eye, whether to trafficking in America or the pain and suffering in

Israel. But it's in these dire circumstances that we need our faith the most. Even if you don't believe in God, faith—this relentless hope that this world can be better and that we can play an active part in its healing—is necessary to adopt. Without this kind of disposition, entering the fight will feel impossible.

You are chosen. You are loved. You are God's workmanship. You were created to do good works. God prepared these works in advance for you to do. But you must *trust* this is the case—that this is indeed your reality. Worthiness isn't important because we *aren't* worthy of God's perfect love. What matters to God is obedience. We are called to respond to Him. As 1 John 4:19 says, "We love because he first loved us." When you begin to see the most vulnerable as chosen, as loved, as deserving of life, liberty, and the pursuit of happiness, your faith will be kept alive, for you'll experience a light radiating from those you've chosen to serve.

Trusting What We Remember

Right after God comes to Moses through the burning bush, we read that Moses protests God's call. Moses argues with God, "Who am I that I should go to Pharaoh and bring the Israelites out of Egypt?" (Exodus 3:11). God comforts Moses with the reminder of the truth of His presence. "I will be with you," Yahweh says (Exodus 3:12). Scholars suggest that Moses was insecure about his speaking abilities, possibly a speech impediment. Scripture seems to indicate that Moses likely stuttered and stammered. And now God was asking Moses to lead a massive people group out of slavery!

Moses continues his protest in the next chapter, "Pardon your servant, Lord. I have never been eloquent, neither in the past nor since you have spoken to your servant. I am slow of speech and tongue" (Exodus 4:10). And again a few verses later, "Pardon your servant, Lord. Please send someone else" (Exodus 4:13).

We can sense that Moses is having something of a crisis of self-worth in the intensity of encountering this divine call. He feels like God is calling him into something that is "in over his head." Maybe he was replaying his past, and that was causing him self-doubt. Moses was content, but now Yahweh was throwing a wrench in that contentment, calling him forth into the unknown.

He was to be a foreigner in a foreign land once again.

Have you ever felt as though your life was unfolding "business as usual," but then something came along and undeniably stirred your heart in a way that required a response to the call you felt? It's in this tension that the enemy will try to attack you. This is when self-doubt tends to rise within you to muffle the call. This is when you may question your self-worth or replay all your past mistakes. Anything that makes you doubt that you are God's workmanship, that you were designed to do good works that God prepared for you, is a lie straight from the pit of hell.

Most of us have experienced the feeling of, "Am I capable and ready for this?" When I first became a general manager, I had confidence in my ability to succeed, but I would sometimes question myself when unusual situations occurred. When I got into the fight against child sex trafficking, I realized I didn't know everything about this evil. I still don't, but I trust that if God called me to do this, He would equip me, mold me, and provide what I need to battle this monster.

All God asks is for a willing, fighting heart.

It doesn't matter where you've been or what you've been—no one can take away the fact that God loves you and wants to do something *in* you and *through* you. As Yahweh says to Moses, "I will be with you." We have the power of the Holy Spirit living inside us but tend to act instead as if we are alone on this journey. We need to remember this truth whenever we doubt our self-worth or divine purpose.

The mystery of God is that He calls you and me to be a part of what He is doing in history. God has chosen us, all of us, to be His hands in doing those things in the world that are important to Him. The Lord is looking for people to stand in the breach, intervene, and seek justice for these people He loves.

Exploitation

The more I delved into learning about the epidemic of human trafficking, the more I discovered that self-worth is precisely what traffickers try to exploit. A predator may sit in a crowded area like a mall and say to young girls, "You are beautiful," or, "Has anyone told you how pretty you are?" If the girl ignores them or says "thanks," the predator won't continue the conversation. But if the girl says, "No, I'm not," or "No one has ever told me I'm pretty," the predator has found their target.

From there, the predator may introduce themselves or offer to buy them something, and, before they know it, they are telling them about a mysterious opportunity where they will always feel beautiful and make lots of money while doing so. The predator will shower them with compliments and praise, making the target feel as special as possible.

For those who have experienced childhood trauma, they are often enticed by the idea of a "family" who will accept them as they are and a "home" where they can rest their heads. Before they know it, they are being asked to do pornography or "work the streets," it doesn't take long for the trafficker to have all the leverage. Suppose the person being trafficked wants to leave the lifestyle. In that case, the trafficker may threaten to upload a sex video to the Internet, hurt their family, or share information with the person's community. This is called "sextortion."

One of the most disgusting things about predators or "groomers" is their radar for people's insecurities and their desire to exploit their pains and traumas. They are master manipulators of the emotions of vulnerable people. They position themselves as a parent-like figure who can make all the person's troubles disappear and manipulate the young person into believing the groomer's promises. In the anti-trafficking community, these are described as Romeo pimps or Gorilla pimps. It is truly baffling that this exists so prominently—and goes overlooked—in a country where most people claim to be Christian. It's upsetting, gross, horrific.

A friend of mine from Los Angeles, a sex-trafficked survivor and thriver, was sold for sex from the ages of eleven to fifteen. Her name is Oree.

She grew up in an environment where she was molested multiple times between the ages of five and eleven, including being raped by a classmate in the second grade. Dealing with an unfathomable amount of pain and confusion, she decided to leave home at eleven years old, seeking safety at a friend's house, which eventually led to her being dropped off at a crack house. Data shows that within forty-eight hours of leaving home, runaways will be approached by a trafficker.

At the crack house, Oree remembers a man named JB approaching her and making her feel more heard than anyone ever had before. He asked her questions about her background. About her family. About why she was in the situation she was in. Before she knew it, Oree was confessing to JB her entire life story. Though she didn't have language for it at the time, she felt the man was meeting a deep unconscious need for her desire to belong, be accepted, be understood, and be home.

"I bet it's been a while since you've showered or changed your clothes," the man said, handing her a black bag. "Get cleaned up, relax. You're safe now."

Next, it was a woman nearby who continued the grooming process. She shared her own story with Oree—how she too, had been molested multiple times by family members and ran from home. She explained to Oree how they were like *real* family at the house, how JB made sure that nothing bad ever happened to them, and how she was about to head to work as an "escort." Oree didn't know what that meant, so the woman explained the nature of her work.

"That sounds like prostitution!" Oree said. "I don't want to do that."

"No, it's not like that," the woman pushed back. "You're already doing this stuff for free when you're home with your family—JB just wants to help us to get paid. And he will make sure that nothing bad ever happens to you."

Oree was hesitant but couldn't help but feel like the woman was right. The crack house *was* way better than where she was coming from. At the crack house, she was told she had protection, housing, food, money, and people who would love and accept her. The woman told her that she would never be forced to do something she didn't want to do. Oree decided to stay.

But, when it came time for her first "assignment," and she protested through uncontrollable tears, JB grabbed her and struck her.

"What are you crying for?" he yelled. "You've gone through too much in your life to cry about some shit like this. You ain't got no f&%$ing home. You ain't got no f&%$ing parents. You don't have nobody."

Then he paused and held her, "After all the shit you've been through, this will be nothing. I've got you. I've got you."

The man had used everything Oree had told him that first night against her. He had made her feel like she had no escape by physically abusing her, but then, almost immediately after, he had given her something she had always craved through his tenderness, embrace, and "support" of her.

Her first "assignment," she'd find out, entailed being trafficked to fourteen men that night.

Oree reflects, "That night, something died in me."

11

HEART TO MIND, MIND TO HEART

"You may choose to look the other way
but you can never say again that you did not know."
~William Wilberforce

As I entered the waters of activism, I knew I had a lot to learn. My heart had been set aflame. Nothing could tamper my conviction. However, I needed to educate myself about the space I was entering. Today, that's where I see a lot of activism go awry. It's all heart, no mind. It's all revolution, no reason. It's all wrath, no wisdom.

Consider this parallel from my experiences as a baseball scout.

The late 80s and early 90s were a unique time to rise through the ranks as a baseball scout because of the influx of data used to formulate an educated projection about a prospect's potential. These were golden years for scouting—when statistics and qualitative observation went hand-in-hand, and these insights complemented one another. These comprehensive stats helped me as a scout, yet they were not the driving force. I would meet players' families, talk to their girlfriends and friends, interview their coaches or teammates, talk to school teachers or counselors—anything I could do to formulate an accurate character assessment of a prospect.

We called this in-depth assessment of a person's character and potential "makeup." We see the stats and have the data, but, quite literally, what is the prospect made of? This involves intangibles like heart, character, integrity, and "coachability."

Mike Piazza, for example, was a guy with *great* makeup. He didn't stand out on the stats sheet coming up as a prospect. One could argue whether he was even a legitimate "prospect." The Dodgers drafted him in the *sixty-second round* of the 1988 MLB amateur draft, where he was the 1,390th player picked out of 1,395 players. It's believed this was done as a favor to Piazza's father, a good friend of Dodgers legend Tommy Lasorda.

All of this is crazy to think about. Piazza, who would become a Hall of Famer, was overlooked by every team in Major League Baseball for sixty-one rounds and possibly only got drafted *because* of his father.

But Piazza worked hard, was coachable, and was determined to play at the Major League level. His makeup was an indicator that he had no ceiling for greatness. With today's emphasis on analytics (mind, if you will), makeup (heart) often gets overlooked, just as in Piazza's case.

In baseball, in life, in fighting for justice, heart and mind cannot be divorced from one another. They must complement each other. Passion and the desire to change the world are great, but they must be married with knowledge and education. Qualitative experience must be matched with quantitative measurements.

Balancing Passion

Jesus had a brilliant mind. The parables he told were subversive. He knew the Hebrew Scriptures, quoting passages that contradicted the religion of the Pharisees and Sadducees. But he also had heart.

In Matthew 21 and Mark 11, we read about a wild scene where Jesus enters the temple of Jerusalem and begins overturning tables of merchants who were selling goods on sacred grounds. Jesus quotes Scripture and says to them, "It is written, 'My house will be called a house of prayer,' but you are making it 'a den of robbers.'"

Jesus was so angry to see the temple turned into a marketplace to see religion used for commerce. This is such a human scene, isn't it?

Even though Jesus was the Son of God, he was not without intense emotion. There are other examples of Jesus's anger, most notably when he became frustrated with the Pharisees and Sadducees, who were using religion for personal gain. There are also a couple of almost shocking times when he snaps at his dear friend, Peter, whom Jesus would later task with starting his church. Jesus experienced intense anguish in the Garden of Gethsemane the night before he was crucified, felt deep sorrow when he encountered the grief of others, discovered radical joy in pleasing his Father, and experienced anything from compassion to exhaustion to frustration in his ministry. There are many other times throughout the gospels where Jesus's emotion is on full display.

Even if you don't believe Jesus was the Son of God or the world's savior, I don't think anyone can deny that Jesus was an activist. He shattered categories that religious people had constructed to exclude others. He was determined to show the world his Father's love and broke religious people's rules while doing so. He was a nuisance to the Roman Empire as he modeled a more loving way to live life and serve others, especially those society had abandoned. He challenged established systems. He disrupted order. People in power didn't know how to categorize him. He was in his own fight against the evils of this world and the oppression these evils caused. At times, he wore his heart on his sleeve. In the rare times he showed anger, it came from a place of love and a desire to help people wake up to their unfulfilled lives.

I find Jesus's emotion comforting. Activists are some of the most emotional people I've met. We are passionate. On a mission. Highly sensitive to the pain in this world. We carry the scars of our efforts and the burdens of the world's darkness. We sometimes struggle to turn off our minds. Our hearts are often in a constant state of grief for those suffering. We can sometimes come across as blunt, perturbed, or angry whenever the suffering of those we are trying to serve goes ignored. We can experience exhilarating highs when we take a big step forward in our fights against injustice and intense lows when we take a step backward or feel that no one cares. I'm reminded by Jesus's example that the goal is not to numb our emotions but to harness them correctly. As Peter Scazarro wrote in his book *Emotionally Healthy Spirituality*, "Ignoring our emotions is turning our back on reality. Listening to our emotions ushers us into reality. And reality is where we meet God."

I sometimes let my emotions lead the way without considering the consequences of my words or actions. I once screamed to one of the Florida governor's chief advisors over the phone, "You just don't care about kids getting trafficked, do you?!?"

My partner John, who ran our boys safe home in Tampa from 2018-2021, called the governor's staff back and apologized, "Kevin didn't mean what he said. He's just really passionate."

But I believe that passion is exactly the thing that can be harnessed to make the world a better place.

Before I knew God, my passion often came out through needless fighting. As a general manager, my bluntness was sometimes endearing to my bosses and the media; other times, it got me into trouble. When trying to advocate for Shawn, my advocating helped him get the best care at three different hospitals, but I also got kicked out of Craig Hospital one night. As an activist, my fiery ways sometimes motivate people to join me in the fight against human trafficking; other times, it is intimidating and might make someone feel paralyzed with guilt or apathy.

In Matthew 12:33-34, Jesus directly connects our speech and heart when he says, "Make a tree good and its fruit will be good, or make a tree bad and its fruit will be bad, for a tree is recognized by its fruit. You brood of vipers, how can you who are evil say anything good? For the mouth speaks what the heart is full of."

In activism, logic, reason, democratization, nuance, and debate—all these matters of the mind—sometimes take a backseat to passion, conviction, and fury (heart). When mind and heart don't balance each other, the effects are often counterproductive. For example, at the 2022 Super Bowl in Los Angeles, a group thought it was a good idea to drive around with vans and try to snatch up girls being trafficked. This "strategy" likely stemmed from the myth that human trafficking is like the movie *Taken*, the action-thriller starring Liam Neeson, a retired CIA agent who uses his skills to rescue his kidnapped daughter. It's hardly ever that way. Trafficking is messy and nuanced. Nonetheless, these "activists" believed abducting victims right off the street was a great plan. This could only result in people getting shot and killed.

Passion, combined with patience and pragmatism, usually has a better chance of inviting others into the fight against injustice.

The 2022 Super Bowl in Los Angeles was special for me in a few ways that had nothing to do with football. You may remember that when I was the General Manager for the Dodgers, the *Los Angeles Times* went after me relentlessly. This time, however, they ran a front-page article on me and my transition from the former Dodgers GM to now fighting child sex trafficking. More importantly, the NFL and the Los Angeles Sports and Entertainment Commission appointed me to be the convener of all anti-human trafficking efforts. I led the the strategic planning months in advance and coordinated with all the anti-human trafficking organizations working to prevent trafficking or provide victim services for those rescued during the week of the Super Bowl.

The results of our collaborative efforts were significant to say the least. A total of seventy adult victims were rescued, and eight minors were recovered. Thirty-four people suspected of trafficking were arrested, as well as 494 sex buyers statewide.

I was offered this opportunity to lead these operations because of my many years of fighting human trafficking in Los Angeles, especially in the gang communities of South Central L.A. I've partnered in battling child sex trafficking for many years with Alfred Lomas, a former gang shot caller who is the Founder and Executive Director of Inner City Visions which included offices in the Florence-Firestone community of Los Angeles.

I think our efforts at the Super Bowl were a reflection of how far I've come in my personal growth. I am still learning to slow down and evaluate—and probably always will—what is in my heart before it comes out through my words. Righteous wrath, I think, is found by having the humility and curiosity to sift through our hearts and minds. As Paul wrote in 2 Corinthians 10:5, "We demolish arguments and every pretension that sets itself up against the knowledge of God, and we take captive every thought to make it obedient to Christ."

To fight for justice is to fight for that which is closest to God's heart. Vulnerable children being exploited and enslaved is surely one of the issues closest to God's heart. God cares deeply about those on the margins of society—those who have been forgotten, neglected, betrayed, and abused, for this was the same state of Jesus Christ on his road to Calvary.

"I Will Help You"

As Moses protests the divine call from the burning bush, insecure about his speaking abilities, Yahweh comforts Moses by saying, "I will help you speak and will teach you what to say" (Exodus 4:12). The fact that Yahweh is going to teach Moses what to say or do invites Moses to adopt a posture of learning. I like this notion when it comes to activism.

When I felt the call to help stop human trafficking, my heart was on fire, but I knew this wasn't enough. I needed to be radically open to learning and educating myself on the nuances and complexities of this layered problem in the United States. In other words, I needed to let God teach me. I needed to thoroughly scout the darkness of this problem before acting upon it. If I could learn about the varying layers of this problem, then I could educate others as well.

In today's polarized landscape, many activists get caught up in the emotion of the moment rather than learning about the complexities of the problem so they can educate others as well. In other words, their passion becomes redirected into an arrogant type of certainty. In Las Vegas, where much of our anti-trafficking activism occurs today, some individuals feel they are the only ones who know how to fight human trafficking. If they're *not* doing what you're doing or didn't *think* of the idea you're proposing, they often try to prevent help from happening. Some of these individuals will attack you personally and even all the good work that has been done. It's often an insecurity they live with that displays itself as arrogance.

What we all saw take place in 2020 is another example of what I'm talking about. After the unlawful killing of George Floyd, we rightfully saw people flood into the streets demanding reform of law enforcement. This brought to the surface issues of racism that still exist in our country today and the need to discuss them. But one of the rallying cries by progressives became three detrimental words to their overall cause: *defund the police*. A noble cause for justice that got American people of all political leanings talking about the ripple effects of racism lost a great deal of respect because of these three words. Data has shown that most African Americans want *more* policing. Many moderates and conservatives became repelled by a meaningful movement. It wasn't long, you might remember, before Americans returned to their divisions and ideological camps.

In 2014, I started Protect the PATH (People Against Trafficking Humans). This organization began primarily to make people aware of human trafficking and educate them on the issues. It was a placeholder to get me started. In 2016, former IBM vice president Geoff Rogers and I began the United States Institute Against Human Trafficking (USIAHT, usiaht.org). I knew Geoff's cerebral and business approach would balance my passion for the fight. At the USIAHT, we frame our fight into four categories: 1) Education (learning), 2) Prevention/Disruption (scouting), 3) Rescue (standing in the gap), and 4) Restoration (healing victims). I believe these four levels are universal in people's justice fights.

Look at some of the great activists like Dr. Martin Luther King Jr. or Mother Teresa. They had a deep awareness of the systemic issues their people faced—they were scouts. They were willing to stand in the gap—they got messy. They served "the least of these" day in and day out, committed to rescuing the downtrodden and rejuvenating their spirits. They made restoration their chief goal. These four quadrants, in my opinion, help balance the heart and mind.

At the USIAHT, we gather metrics and measurements, and create dashboards and KPIs to help explain how to fight human trafficking. We believe in results. We identify technological and geographic trends. We formulate and test theories, always looking for best practices and utilizing third-party analysis. For example, as we today seek to confront human sex trafficking in an effective way in southern Nevada, we hired a renowned research team at the University of Nevada-Reno to compile a gap analysis on human sex trafficking in Las Vegas and Clark County. Their one-hundred-page report in 2023 was shocking, and the results are now available. Because of this report, we were able to add and change laws, as well as create and open thirty-six recovery beds for trafficked girls.

In Clark County, its economic dependence on tourism, the national perception that all is permissible in Vegas (hence, the city slogan "What happens in Vegas, stays in Vegas!"), as well as the weak legal punishments that would hold buyers ("Johns") and traffickers ("Pimps") more accountable, were all issues that conflated to create such a horrific human sex trafficking problem in Southern Nevada. According to Shared Hope International, Nevada's grade in their 2022 Human Trafficking Report is an "F." The study's researchers conclude that awareness, prevention, and education are vital in Southern Nevada if the state ever hopes to raise its abysmal grade in human trafficking.

One of my primary objectives is to get training and curriculum into the schools. We believe junior high (6th, 7th, and 8th graders) is the best age for students to begin learning about human trafficking and empower them to recognize predators in their and their friends' lives. Awareness is the start and the key to any kind of prevention.

Into the Heart

We also did research on human trafficking in the state of Florida. Though Florida ranked well according to Shared Hope International's annual report cards (which gauge criminal provisions, identification of and response to victims, continuum of care, access to justice for trafficking survivors, tools for a victim-centered criminal justice response, and prevention/training), we realized there was a massive gap in services for young boys who had been trafficked.

Did you know that twenty-five percent of sex trafficking victims are children, and, according to a recent Department of Justice study, up to *thirty-six percent* of these American children are *young boys?* Almost four out of ten children trafficked in the United States are boys. People mistakenly thought in Florida that human sex trafficking primarily involved young girls. So, for four years in Florida, we operated the only safe home in the country for trafficked boys. Thirty-four boys received care and wraparound services during those four years.

Often, boys go completely under the radar because we don't tend to view boys as victims. Think about it. To better understand the differing sexual ethics we have for boys and girls, it may help to consider this unfortunately common scenario. When a male teacher has sex with one of his female high school students, we want justice for the girl. We tend to rightfully view her as a victim who the teacher manipulated and coerced into doing something in which she could not possibly understand the consequences. However, when a female teacher has sex with one of her male high school students, the boy is often applauded and praised. In other words, we see the girl as a helpless victim who needs rescuing and the boy as a man capable of making his own decisions.

Time and again, when we talk to trafficked boys, they hang their heads and tell us, "If I told anyone what I was being forced to do, they wouldn't believe me." I can certainly relate to this sense of brokenness. For decades, I told no one about what the priest did to me. Oddly, I didn't see myself as a victim. I saw myself as possibly responsible. Similarly, most trafficked boys are forced to perform homosexual acts, heightening and complicating the victim's shame and confusion.

Our own education—our openness to being taught, "coached," and most importantly, learning from the victims themselves—has positioned us to educate others. For example, at the beginning of President Donald Trump's administration, Geoff and I sought to advocate (not lobby, but educate) for widespread policy changes within the highest levels of the United States government. You may be wondering: Isn't a department already doing that? To most people's surprise, the State Department only focuses on *international* trafficking. Until we made them aware of the need, there had never been an office or position that focused solely on domestic trafficking.

We wanted the government to enact harsher penalties for buyers and traffickers, to create a full-time human trafficking position at the White House for someone who would focus solely on trafficking in the United States, and to enact a human trafficking advisory board that would provide feedback about policy through a trafficking lens for the White House. My extensive network from being a general manager in MLB and Geoff's professional experience of serving as one of the youngest vice presidents at IBM, often landed us a meeting and usually warranted a response. Our backgrounds got us in the door.

It took a while, and was sometimes frustrating to crack through the bureaucratic shell of Washington, D.C. Still, we eventually met with Vice President Mike Pence's policy advisor, Sarah

Makin. We met in the Eisenhower Executive Building, next door to the White House. Our business approach to such a complex problem blew her and Vice President Pence's staff away. After all, trafficking was a thriving business, so it would take business principles to help take it down. Geoff was great at explaining our metrics, measurements, and business structure. I like to think I was good at reading the room and igniting people's hearts to fight this terrible problem. In a sense, we were the perfect combination of heart and mind for a task like that. It truly felt like we were anointed for these kinds of meetings. At the end of the session, we began to talk with Sarah about faith. When I asked her if she would tell us about her faith, she began to cry. She said no one had ever asked her to share something like that in a meeting.

Our success with Vice President Pence's staff led to another meeting with Ivanka Trump and her staff. We met with Ivanka in the White House, and I broke the ice by telling her about my activism with Israel as a Christian Zionist. Ivanka and her husband, Jared, are Jewish. We then launched into our presentation. It was never rehearsed, by the way. We wanted it to come straight from our hearts. In fact, Geoff and I would pray before every meeting, asking God to speak through us and open the hearts of those we were speaking to.

Like Sarah Makin, Ivanka Trump didn't take long to get on board. We occasionally corresponded via email, and she and her staff became instrumental in developing a Public/Private Partnership to End Domestic Human Trafficking, on which I was asked to serve. Thanks to the work of her and her staff, on January 31, 2020, President Trump signed an executive order for federal legislation to combat trafficking, which included the largest Department of Justice grant package to fight trafficking. The order also created the Center for Countering Human Trafficking within the Department of Homeland Security so that there was a centralized location for combatting trafficking. That this position created under Trump has been unfilled under President Joe Biden is frustrating.

Let me say it loud and clear: there is *no reason* why combatting human sex trafficking should be a partisan issue.

I believe we can stop human sex trafficking in the United States. But it starts with an openness to learning, in which bureaucrats in D.C. tend to fail. As God said to Moses, "I will teach you." Are we willing to dare hear the voice of God on issues that we may not understand?

At USIAHT, we are determined to take our education-based model into the pits of darkness and meet that darkness head-on. If we educate parents and young people about the grooming process, they may be able to recognize perpetrators or, God forbid, someone targeting their own son or daughter. If we educate individuals on what to look for when they are out in public, we may see more reports to law enforcement and save children everywhere from having a night like Oree had where she felt like everything within her died. No one—*no one*—should have to experience that kind of hopelessness and despair.

Sometimes, the task feels overwhelming, like when a breakthrough suddenly feels like it's all for nothing once a new administration comes in, but we are determined. The great thing about striving to marry aspects of the heart and mind within ourselves and our mission is that we have a better chance of opening the hearts and minds of others—and what God may want us to do next.

I will teach you.

Will each of us allow ourselves to be taught? Will we work together to truly make a difference?

The Bible teaches that God loves justice and hates injustice, and His anger is roused by evil, and it rests on evildoers. God is moved with compassion toward all who suffer.

Many Christians claim to know God—they can quote Scripture, theology, and apologetics. But I believe our passion for justice and defense of the weak *truly* reflect how well we know God, for God is a God of justice. We read in Isaiah 1:17 that God calls His people to "seek justice, rescue the oppressed, defend the orphan, and plead for the widow." We are called to hear the orphan's plea, be challenged, and do something about it. Our young trafficked victims are our modern-day orphans.

12
INHERENT POTENTIAL

"We are not to simply bandage the wounds of victims beneath the wheels of injustice, we are to drive a spoke into the wheel itself."
-Dietrich Bonhoeffer

As a scout, the biggest thing I was looking for every game or practice I watched was *potential*. I had to be aware of upcoming talent and to communicate to my supervisors how and why I thought a particular player would be a good fit (or *could* be a good fit in the future) on our Major League roster to help us win world championships. Projecting a player's future Major League production and the reasoning why is way more difficult than you'd think.

For example, the goal was to not only target who I thought was the best player coming up (or the best five players, for that matter) because our first-round selection might not be until the twentieth pick. So, my goal as a scout would be to project what players would be best for us to draft when our picks came around. In other words, my awareness of upcoming talent had to be so deep that I could accurately predict who would be taken in earlier rounds and who would still be available to select when our pick came along. I was looking for prospects with the *most* potential based on the range in which I projected they would be drafted.

Scouts could earn a lot of credibility by accurately predicting which round or pick certain players would fall and thus be able to provide the *best* recommendations for realistic picks to their organizations. This was how organizations could gain an edge over other teams. If their scouts were correct about a prospect's potential, particularly one that no other organization was high on or targeting, then the organization's overall talent was deepening while others remained stagnant. This helped build up their farm system and also provided them with trade leverage in case they wanted to make a move for someone else in the future, like a veteran player, to win now. The best scouts could accurately predict what players had the best long-term potential based on tools, makeup, and performance.

There was a real rush in seeing a player's potential that no one else seemed to see, then advocating for that player to one's superiors. You hoped you were right because your job was on the line if you weren't. It was even more of a rush when that player excelled within the organization, climbed through the farm system, and contributed in a big way on the MLB level. Scouts may not get the same credit as general managers who make big moves that attract headlines, but their jobs are just as important, if not more so. An organization's strength and health depend on its scouting department and the pipeline of talent it has created for player development. Most organizations, after all, just can't go out and buy a bunch of All-Stars. We learned this the hard way in Montreal. By the time our guys had developed into All-Stars, we could no longer afford them.

What was most fulfilling as a scout was to see a young man be selected in the recommended round and excel at the next level. Two of those guys for me were a catcher named Tim Laker (taken by the Expos in the sixth round in 1988) and Bret Barberie (drafted in the 7th round of that same year by the Expos), who would both become starters within the next few years. My core job as a scout was to see potential and accurately project when we should draft them.

Speaking of potential, I remember in 1995, when I was the Expos General Manager, we drafted a six-foot-three, one-hundred-and-ninety pound left-handed hitting catcher in the 18th round of the MLB Amateur Draft. He was also a pretty good high school football player, and we did everything possible to sign this prospect from Junipero Serra High School in San Mateo, California. That summer while I was traveling with our Major League team we went into San Francisco to play the Giants. I asked our Expos area scout, John Hughes, to bring this catcher to Candlestick Park before our game so we could work him out.

This prospect was quiet, shy, and a young man of few words. We knew he wasn't fast so there was no need to time him in the sixty-yard dash. He got my attention though with his very smooth swing, which demonstrated excellent power potential. He also had soft hands when receiving the baseball, as well as a strong and accurate arm for throwing out future base stealers in Major League Baseball. This high school catcher was projected to be a productive offensive catcher, potentially hitting twenty-five to thirty home runs per season, a skillset hard to find in pro catchers. Combine all that with his above-average defensive abilities and his cerebral skills—which indicated to us that he was a leader who would be able to call an excellent game in working with and handling a pitching staff—we determined he could and would become a Major League All-Star catcher. We offered this prospect second round money, which was substantial.

His heart, however, was set on playing college football. He signed with the University of Michigan and was eventually drafted by the New England Patriots in the sixth round of the NFL draft. He'd go on to win seven Super Bowls and three NFL MVPs. The prospect's name was Tom Brady. I think he made the right choice sticking with football.

So, what does all of this have to do with purpose, with justice?

Matthew 25 has a famous parable that Jesus shared, often called "The Sheep and the Goats" parable. In this parable, Jesus identifies what it truly means to live a righteous, purposeful life by juxtaposing those who sat on their ivory tower of fraudulent righteousness with those who loved their neighbor and served those who needed help. God will separate those two groups of people in the afterlife, Jesus says, just like a shepherd separates sheep from goats. Jesus then makes the outstanding claim that those who served "the least of these" in their lifetimes were *also* serving him, the King of Glory. As he says in Matthew 25:35-36, "For I was hungry and you gave me something to eat, I was thirsty and you gave me something to drink, I was a stranger and you invited me in, I needed clothes and you clothed me, I was sick and you looked after me, I was in prison and you came to visit me."

To be a scout is to realize that everyone has inherent potential, no matter their plight. To be a scout is to single them out and help them to bring their dreams to fruition. To scout the enemy is to realize that anytime we are blinded from seeing the inherent potential of another person and thus refuse to help them, we have bought into the lies of the evil one.

Satan wants us to lead lives disconnected from the suffering of the world. He wants us to be isolated. He wants us to focus all our time and energy on fulfilling our selfish desires. All of this helps pain and suffering flourish, leading people to doubt God's goodness. Jesus, on the other hand, wants us to see *him* in the least of these, in the forgotten, in the outcasts, in those the world has labeled as "other" or worthless.

To be a scout, to live a life anchored in purpose and justice, is to see the image of God in every person and do what we can to cultivate that image. It is to see potential and help them to see it, too.

Better, Not Bitter

Brandy Crisafulli, founder and president of Life Recaptured, has created a safe place for survivors where she offers women trapped in sexual exploitation a path toward refuge and freedom.

Brandy and her younger sister grew up with an abusive father. When Brandy learned in 2014 that, in the chaos of their upbringing, her sister had been trafficked by a "family friend," she became outraged, consumed by a rage that derailed her life and sense of well-being.

It had been decades. Brandy wondered how she had never known what this man was doing. How could she seek justice years after the fact when there was no physical evidence of what he had done? Seeking revenge was all she thought about. This man went on living his life without consequence, while her sister would forever carry the weight of the trauma *he* caused.

I have encountered many situations like this, where I am overwhelmed by the injustice of a situation. I'm a fighter. That inner rage doesn't just go away. I have long been involved with the Los Angeles Dream Center and have developed deep relationships with gang leaders in the Los Angeles area as we strive to help meet the needs of the communities where these gangs operate. (These needs, by the way, are often what some gangs are also trying to meet, albeit illegally.) On several occasions, I've had a gang leader learn about a situation and offer to "take care of it." I admit, there have been times when I've been so infuriated that I've been tempted to say yes. I can't imagine how angry I'd be if I learned that one of my family members or friends was trafficked for years without my knowledge. Brandy is a hero of mine.

Brandy says she eventually prayed to God, "How do I get over this anger?" Her anger, she says, was killing her.

She felt that God responded, "How about you help others?"

In other words, get better, not bitter. Brandy felt God was saying she should make the world a *better* place rather than let bitterness fester and rot her from the inside out.

Brandy began educating herself about the proper care for women who have been trafficked, exploited, and abused.

In 2019, Brandy opened a Florida safe home called Life Recaptured that has served hundreds of women who found themselves in situations just like her sister had years before. We began supporting her through the USIAHT. One of the goals at USIAHT is to be a hub for combatting human trafficking, where we educate people on this problem but also partner with organizations we've screened who are preventing trafficking, interrupting trafficking, or restoring victims in a way that we believe addresses the core needs of this fight. We want people to be able to support us and, in doing so, know that we will support—financially and in other ways—the most effective organizations and nonprofits that meet the darkness of human trafficking head-on.

Every day, her safe home receives calls from family members, lawyers, or law enforcement, seeking safety and recovery for someone they have worked with. Brandy's safe home brings them in to assess their physical, mental, and emotional needs. Then they seek to meet that person where they are, wherever they are, for however long their recovery takes. There is no perfect formula or prescription for healing trauma. We would not partner with organizations advocating for a "quick fix."

Most of the time, this rehabilitation takes extremely long, often forever. Most young women Brandy works with have little trust in humanity. They've been treated as an object for so long that they think everyone is out to get them. Brandy has been bitten, spit on, and cursed out countless times. But she and her staff commit themselves again and again to unconditional, patient, and consistent love. This, as Francis Chan says in "Advocate"— our five-episode educational series for churches about human trafficking (advocateseries.com)—is eventually recognized as "real love" when it is compared to the coercive, manipulative "love" they have experienced in the past.

Brandy recently encountered a young woman who was in terrible physical shape. She had been raped and abused several times that day. They called the hospital, where the victim spent twelve straight days recovering. Doctors told Brandy that had the woman gotten to the hospital two hours later, she likely would have died. The woman spent over a year in Brandy's safe home, reconstructing her life and sense of worth.

"I've never been loved like this," the woman told Brandy one day.

Holy Ground

Sometimes, the work we do to fight human trafficking can feel overwhelming. The darkness we confront in the human condition every day can be unfathomable. It can get you down. It can make you feel like that famous image of the Greek god endlessly pushing that boulder up a mountain, only for it to roll back down again each time it nears the top. Right when we make progress or have a significant breakthrough, a new battle seems to arise.

But I think it's important to continually come back to our conviction for what is right and wrong. I knew that day as a nine-year-old when I went after the guys making fun of my uncle that there was no other option but to fight for this person I loved. When I get down about the world's darkness, I try to return to my fundamental conviction to fight for the people we love.

In Exodus 3:5-6, Yahweh asks Moses to take off his sandals before the burning bush because he is standing on "holy ground." I think it was holy ground not only because of God's presence, but also because of what God was calling Moses to do. In the next verse is Yahweh's declaration that He has "seen the misery of my people in Egypt and "heard them crying out because of their slave drivers." Moses stood on holy ground, for it was in that very place that Yahweh called out to him to lead the Israelites out of slavery. Yahweh was inviting Moses to *see* and *hear* what Yahweh heard: to notice how the Israelites had been objectified and commodified by the powerful and to *do* something about it. There is no call as holy and sacred as this.

As you read this, you may be thinking, "I'm not close to God. I don't know if God is saying anything to me...I don't know if I'm called in the same way." Okay, when you hear about kids being sold for sex, what do you think and feel? Do you feel *empathy*, the ability to identify or understand another's situation or feelings? Do you feel *compassion*, the ability to feel another person's pain, and wanting to take steps to relieve their suffering? If so, this is exactly what I felt. God is calling you, too—not to do everything but to do something. *That's* the invitation.

No matter whether you are a justice advocate, artist, or a nine-to-five worker in a corporate job, we are called to help others see their inherent potential and to validate their worth. To mirror to them their value. To remind them how loved and accepted they are, even in failure, difficulty, and frustration. As a scout, your job is to help people to unearth their potential. If they can't see it, then you have to *help* them see it. In this context, scouting the enemy means assisting people to become aware of all the lies and voices in their lives that don't positively cultivate their potential.

As you pursue purpose and justice, as you try to make this world a better place, there will be stories that shake you to the core. There will be moments when you, like Moses, stand paralyzed in your tracks, protesting to God what He is calling you to do. But remember that you are on holy ground. The Creator of the Universe called *you* forth to *be* with Him and *do* something to help heal the world.

Gaze upon the bright light of the flames. Take off your sandals.

13
THE CRUX OF THE LIE

"Make a career of humanity. Commit yourself to the noble struggle for equal rights. You will make a better person of yourself, a greater nation of your country, and a finer world to live in."
-Dr. Martin Luther King Jr.

As a scout and general manager, I often felt the pressure to define a player or coach solely by their statistics or performance. Part of this is the reality of the cutthroat industry that is sports. Maybe you can relate in your line of work. You define people by what you can *measure*: by their quarterly profits, by the deals they landed, by their productivity, efficiency, etc. It's not that these things are unimportant. They are. As much as I'd like to assemble a team based on character alone, this would be a disservice to players and fans alike, who both want to win—winning and performance matter.

The key, however, is not to *define* people by their performance. I learned that trading a player or firing a coach could still include an affirming conversation in their departure, that a difficult talk about performance could still include asking about their family, connecting with them on a deeper level, or even praying with them.

On a road trip to San Francisco to play the Giants, I heard

that All-Star Gary Sheffield was experiencing some personal challenges. I wanted to show him that, as the General Manager of the Dodgers, I not only cared about him as a productive player but as a *person*—with a heart, mind, soul, ideas, dreams, and struggles—who was on a journey. I wanted him to know I cared about him and wanted what was best for him on and off the field. I went to his hotel room, and we both got on our knees and prayed.

Those were the moments that reminded me what being an MLB general manager was all about. Ironically, in the thick of my workaholism with the Dodgers—as I grasped for control trying to "put out fires" and "crack the code"—several opportunities arose to help people in the community. I had the unique opportunity as a General Manager in the nation's second-largest city to, with a simple "yes," arrange for a cancer-stricken child to meet a movie star who would be at the game, or partner with the LA Dream Center to raise awareness about a particular cause, or connect the players with underprivileged youth in the community. Those opportunities always seemed to shake me from my sleep and remind me what life was really about.

But then we'd suffer a losing streak, or I'd read another negative story in the press or have organizational drama, and I would again move into the "performance" hamster wheel. On a hamster wheel, you just go around and around, and no matter how hard or fast you run, it's not enough to get you off the wheel.

Honestly, I defined *myself* by what I could measure, even as a Christian! This is the tendency, it seems, of most American men. From a Christian standpoint, we tend to place our identity in what we *do* rather than who we *are* in Christ. We put our identity in what the *world* says about us rather than what *God* says about us. If our organization was doing well, winning games, making money, and building toward a championship, I could justify my efforts with data indicating our success. However, if our rebuild was slow, then I spiraled down into workaholism. There is, no doubt, a fine line between work ethic/determination and placing your identity in your work, in what you do, and thus, in the *results* of your efforts.

What people don't realize—what *I* didn't know at that time—is that this kind of self-perception is a kind of objectification. Those ungodly long hours I spent at the office at the expense of my family were because I essentially had reduced my identity to my performance. When you objectify yourself, you have more of a tendency to objectify others. In other words, to only see people for what they can do for you rather than what you could do for them.

Today's technology and social media have made dehumanizing or objectifying one another easier. In sports, fans can hide behind their keyboard and avatar as they name-call, scapegoat, or make personal attacks and threats to an athlete, coach, or General Manager. Awful things are tweeted at athletes that fans would never dare say to someone's face. Sports betting has led to increased objectification as well. Rather than enjoying watching a sporting event, we hope to *use* these athletes for our financial gain as fans. This is the trend in many corporate spaces as well. This emphasis on production and the "bottom line" leads to treating workers as machines instead of humans with souls.

Technology has perhaps helped us stay more connected with those we know, but has also made it easier for us to caricature and dehumanize those we disagree with. At their best, social media sites are forums for staying connected to family and friends and exchanging diverse ideas. However, these sites have mostly devolved into people dunking on one another and reducing each other to their ideas, beliefs, or mistakes. Many sites have become a toxic form of communication.

We have overall lost our spiritual connectedness with one another. We are all made in the image of God. We are all loved by the Creator of the universe. Christ died for *all*. But it seems to me that we *use* one another to benefit ourselves. This is the definition of objectification. And it's getting us nowhere as a society.

Objectification is also at the very crux of the evil that is human sex trafficking.

Savanna's Story

Savanna's parents were alcoholics and drug addicts. By the age of five, Savanna's neighbor began abusing her sexually. Her parents did not want to call the cops because they did not want law enforcement to find out that they were selling and using drugs. Evidence of their activity was all over the house.

Her mother's drug addiction worsened. By the age of eight, her mom began taking Savanna to a nearby bar and leaving her in the car. When her mother left the bar with another man, Savanna would have to walk home in the late hours of the night. Savanna didn't realize that her mother was prostituting herself to fuel her drug addiction.

Savanna once went with her mother to her drug dealer's house. She did not want to stay home because she never knew when her mother would return. But on that day, her mother's drug dealer offered her a free pinch of crack cocaine if he could have Savanna instead. Her mother agreed—anything for the drugs.

The drug dealer began trafficking Savanna twice a week. He was profiting off of Savanna, and her mother had a constant supply of drugs. Savanna got pregnant twice. She had two abortions. She was not even thirteen years old.

When her parents tried to commit suicide, Savanna was placed in foster care. At one of the group homes, she learned that those who worked there were friends with her trafficker. She continued to be trafficked.

It took the guidance counselor at her high school—a kind woman who could tell that much more was going on in Savanna's life than she was sharing—offering her a place to stay throughout the rest of high school for the cycle of trafficking to stop. But still, anytime Savanna's path crossed with her mother, she would end up getting trafficked once again.

It's easy to think to oneself, *Quit having a relationship with your mom,* but that's the thing about groomers: they are master manipulators. It might surprise you just how much grooming takes place in people's families to fuel addictions or fix financial problems. When Savanna was in high school, her mother explained that she wanted to commit suicide because she hated Savanna and no longer wanted anything to do with her. Since that moment, Savanna began agreeing to anything her mother asked of her, afraid it would be *her* fault if her mom killed herself.

"It was bad, but I would do anything to make my mother want me," Savanna reflects.

When Savanna went to counseling in college and began attending a support group for sexual assault victims, she realized that for over a decade, her mother had been trafficking her. Like most people, Savanna thought that human traffickers were kidnappers who swiped up kids in a van. What she learned is that it is often more subtle. It happens in the shadows, right in front of our eyes. She was trafficked for over a decade and had no idea that was what was happening to her. All she wanted was a normal, loving relationship with her mother, but instead she was trafficked by a master manipulator in the most formative years of her life. That cycle of abuse is difficult to break. And so are those patterns in the mind that revolve around being treated as an object, a commodity, or as someone who can be traded for drugs.

As human beings, we are created to love and be loved. When those responsible for loving us choose the path of abuse instead, it leaves a void that often lasts a lifetime. It takes a lot of love even to begin to fill that void that was left. Many victims of human sex trafficking cannot see beyond the cloud of their trauma and recognize how they've been treated as an object. Because they can't see their potential, they can't trust it. This is one of the reasons why some victims of sex trafficking often find themselves sliding back into that "lifestyle" repeatedly. Their self-worth is so depleted that they are blinded to what life can be. After years of being objectified, they only naturally accept that they are nothing more than an object.

No one should have to carry the pain of going through life thinking they are an object or commodity. To scout the enemy is to combat the dark lies of objectification with the truths of unconditional love and acceptance.

Playing Our Part

Sometimes, the complexities of human trafficking can be overwhelming, but an easy way to fight trafficking is to abstain from pornography. We tend to think of watching porn as a victimless crime, but it's not. Regular porn use leads to the *deterioration* of the mind, *desensitization* of sex, *disembodiment*, and *disconnectedness*. Porn often leads to more extreme fantasies to replicate the same rush, not unlike hard drugs. Porn also fools young, impressionable people with formative minds into thinking that sexual violence or other self-centered fantasies are normal aspects of sex.

Traffickers often force vulnerable children or women into pornography to gain psychological leverage over them. Many of the boys at our safe house told us that they would be forced to watch porn so they could mimic sexual acts or would be threatened by their trafficker that photos or videos would be uploaded to the Internet or sent to a friend or family member if they tried to break free. It is impossible to estimate how much pornography online is some form of sextortion.

Pimps do the same with trafficked victims. Most traffickers generate their clientele via the Internet through videos and photos. In 2022 alone, there was a 105% increase in the online recruitment of mothers. Someone "choosing" to do consensual "sex work" in Southern Nevada doesn't mean they're acting alone as a "freelancer"—often, they are connected to a Pimp who also has his hands in the trafficking of children. Remember, the only difference between prostitution and trafficking is age. Some might disagree with me here, but based on what we've seen in our prevention work with USIAHT, I'm convinced that decreasing pornography use would inevitably reduce trafficking. We tend to think that "sex work" (like prostitution) is a choice someone has made, but then why do ninety percent of women in that "industry" wish they could get out?

Ultimately, this is a supply and demand issue. Because of the slap-on-the-wrist punishments in our legal system, we have to work extra hard to impact demand. Intervention and prevention are complicated. If you lessen demand, then the supply shrinks. Child pornography increased from 45 million Internet images in 2018 to 69.1 million in 2019. I'm told this has grown even more during the isolation of the pandemic.

These dark corners of the Internet might feel removed from your lived experience, but my guess is that either you or someone you know has been impacted by porn use in some way. One in five mobile searches are for pornography. There are nearly 30,000 people consuming porn every second. At the very least, in our hyper-sexualized society, you at least have felt the temptation to search for pornography. Each of us must take responsibility for our actions and refine our minds. As Paul wrote in Philippians 4:8, "Finally, brothers and sisters, whatever is true, whatever is noble, whatever is right, whatever is pure, whatever is lovely, whatever is admirable—if anything is excellent or praiseworthy—think about such things."

Porn is none of these things.

Dehumanization and objectification begin in the mind. I'm not saying that watching porn is anywhere close to the horrors of paying for sex with a child. What I *am* saying is that watching porn often elevates the industry in which traffickers are involved.

To de-objectify is to make the connection to one's heart and mind that the pixelated image on a screen, or the person dancing on a pole, or the person scantily clad on the street corner is *actually* someone's child, parent, family member, friend, and, most importantly, a beloved child of God with a story.

Luke 7:36-50 is the story of the sinful woman pouring perfume on Jesus as he visits the house of a Pharisee. Many believe this was Mary Magdalene, as John proclaims in his gospel, who washed Jesus's feet with her tears, valuable perfume, and hair. In every gospel account, this action by the "sinful woman" was met with criticism that Jesus refuted. In one account, it's Judas accompanying Jesus and ridiculing the woman. In another, it is the apostles. In this account, it is the Pharisee.

The Pharisee struggles to see beyond this woman's past, her social status, her sin, and perhaps what she was wearing. Jesus, on the other hand, sees past it all. He sees her for who she is, a beloved daughter of God who is not defined by her past, her sin, what society has labeled her, or the opinions of the religious leader sitting in the room with them. If stories about Mary's sexual promiscuity are true, we may assume in this scene that one of the things that brought Mary to tears as Jesus spoke was the realization that she was loved, that she was not an object or commodity. Jesus, with a gracious heart, received her gift. Despite her past, he saw Mary for the fullness of who she was.

A Transforming Ethic

As Moses fights Yahweh's call in Exodus 3 and Exodus 4, doubting his ability to do what God has called him to do, Yahweh helps Moses to see beyond his past, his sin, his stammer, his insecurity, and certainly his situation—the fact that he was yet to rekindle his Hebrew roots (as he had fled to Midian), was married to a non-Israelite woman and was likely not even circumcised—one of the religious requirements of that day for the Hebrew people. And now God was calling *him* to free the Israelites?

Perhaps you can understand why Moses felt insecure about leading this new mission. But then and there, before the burning bush, on that holy ground, Yahweh displays what His intimate relationship would be like moving forward: Moses honestly expressing himself to Yahweh, and Yahweh honestly expressing Himself to Moses.

When we are struggling to trust the path ahead, we need to remind ourselves who God is. "I am who I am," Yahweh tells Moses (Exodus 3:14). "This is what you are to say to the Israelites: 'I am has sent me to you.'" These reminders of who God is also help to remind us of who *we* are in Him. We are made for a purpose, created to use the gifts and talents that *He* has given us to make this world a better place and inform people about eternity with God!

As Moses continues to express his hesitancy about the mission, God asks Moses to throw his staff on the ground, which then turns into a snake (Exodus 4:4-5). Next, God tells Moses to place his hand inside his cloak. Moses's hand becomes leprous and is immediately healed when he puts it back in his cloak (Exodus 4:6-7).

We need to recognize how much bigger God is than our problems or insecurities. This alone should allow us to get "outside of ourselves"—freed from the entrapments of our pasts, insecurities, or our low perception of ourselves. We can see in Yahweh's exchange with Moses that He is trying to give Moses the confidence to reconnect to the suffering around him, to perhaps reignite that heart of his that was once so convicted upon witnessing the Israelites' suffering that Moses killed an Egyptian guard.

The Egyptians were treating the Israelite slaves as objects, as a means to an end, and God's connection to Moses opened his eyes to see his connection to human suffering. This ethos that people are made in the image of God and thus should not be treated as objects would transform human history.

14
SCOUTING THE ENEMY

"There may be times when we are powerless to prevent injustice, but there must never be a time when we fail to protest."
~Elie Wiesel

When I was a scout for the Minnesota Twins, I was tasked with scouting the Atlanta Braves for the last eighteen games of the 1991 regular season, and post season, just in case we faced the Braves in the World Series. My job was to do everything I could to equip the Twins to win in case they faced each other. I needed to understand their personnel, strategy, strengths, and weaknesses. I needed to know pitchers' tendencies and temperaments and how to exploit their habits. I needed to do my best to get inside their Manager's head based on the decisions I saw him make. Might he make similar decisions against us? What did he do in high-pressure situations? When did he look to the bullpen? What made him different from other managers?

I needed to evaluate every batter's at-bat and consider what pitches led to them striking out or getting a hit. Were there pitches a batter struggled with? Were there pitches that baited particular batters into swinging? I needed to take all the data I gathered statistically and anecdotally, qualitatively and quantitatively, and identify trends to help us understand what the Braves might do against us.

I also tried to identify similarities the opponents of the Braves might have to our team. How was their team comparable to ours? If I were the General Manager of the Braves, what would I highlight as voids that needed filling? We might need to exploit those voids strategically if we played them.

Maybe you're beginning to see why my scouting report was about two hundred pages long. And we haven't even scratched the surface!

When the Twins did indeed face the Braves in the World Series, our manager Tom Kelly, who we called "TK," asked me to join the team in the Metrodome locker room before Game 1. "You guys have any questions for Kevin about his report?" TK asked the semicircle of players gathered around him. This may sound strange, but it really did happen.

Jack Morris, who would win three games for us in the World Series, asked me who their first-pitch fastball hitters were. I told him. Kirby Puckett, one of the best players in the game at the time, asked me which hitters he should shift defensively and play more in the gaps. I told him. As a young scout, I thought that experience was pretty cool. Scouts didn't attend many Major League games unless they had Major League assignments. I spent most of my time scouting high school, college, and minor league teams. Meeting with the team before Game 1 and sharing the knowledge I had gained from scouting the Braves was an unbelievable experience.

That World Series was a seven-game contest. *Five* of those games were decided by one run. *Three* of those games went into extra innings. It seemed like every little thing we gained from scouting the Braves mattered. Maybe they only used one paragraph of my two-hundred-page report. They might have only used ten pages, or they used it all. Perhaps the Twins *had* to use it all to even stand a chance. In Game 6 or 7, I remember watching the game on television with my family at home and noticing TK pick up my scouting report and look for something. That was cool to see.

I have no idea what they used, didn't use, or whether any of it was helpful. All I know is that every little thing matters—in sports, and in justice work. The Twins ended up defeating the Braves 1-0 in the tenth inning of Game 7 to win its second World Series championship since relocating to Minneapolis in 1961.

As incredible as that experience was, the legwork was grueling. Remember, when I was scouting the Braves, we may have been projected to make the playoffs, but we had no idea how far we'd go, assuming we finished the regular season strong and advanced to the postseason. And we had no idea who we would play in the World Series *if* we even got there. So many things must go your way to make a run in October. If sports betting were a thing back then, there would probably be less than a ten percent chance that the Twins would meet the Braves in the World Series. Other scouts were assigned to compile reports on other teams we could meet. At the beginning of the season, our odds of winning the World Series were 100 to 1.

It didn't matter, however, how slim the chances were in September that the Twins would meet the Braves in the World Series in late October. On my assignment, I had to treat every game, every *pitch*, as if our fate with the Braves was secured. That's the kind of seriousness the task required. If every personnel assigned to scouting a team applied the fullness of their mind to the assignment, then maybe we could be better prepared than any other team when a particular opportunity arose.

I needed to know the Braves like the back of my hand, the way Moses probably understood the palace hallways and personalities of people in Pharaoh's family. There was no intervention—liberation—without scouting the enemy.

Scouts and Spies

In the thirteenth chapter of Numbers, there is an interesting story about the Israelites journeying through the wilderness after leaving Egypt. God asked Moses to send twelve spies to scout the land of Canaan for forty days. Before departing for their mission, Moses told them, "Go up through the Negev and on into the hill country. See what the land is like and whether the people who live there are strong or weak, few or many. What kind of land do they live in? Is it good or bad? What kind of towns do they live in? Are they unwalled or fortified? How is the soil? Is it fertile or poor? Are there trees in it or not? Do your best to bring back some of the fruit of the land" (Numbers 13:17-20).

After forty days, the spies returned with a report of their exploration. They confirm that the land was fruitful, flowing "with milk and honey." But, ten of the spies were overcome with a fear of the powerful people who dwelled in the areas they scouted. They reported that the people were larger and stronger—that they, the Israelites, were mere "grasshoppers" in those people's eyes.

In Numbers 14, Joshua and Caleb—two of the ten spies—encouraged the Israelites to trust God and take the land. Fear reined, however, and the Israelite army talked of stoning Joshua and Caleb (14:10). God punished the Israelites for not trusting Him despite all the miracles He performed to lead them out of Egypt, and made them wander the desert for forty years, until the last spy died.

What's the point of this story? After growing in personal awareness and communicating that awareness to others, we must *trust* our efforts. When I handed over that two-hundred-page scouting report to my boss, I had to trust that my work would help us win. I couldn't control if we won the World Series. All I could control was that month I spent scouting the Braves, doing my assignment with excellence each day.

More importantly, we Christians need to trust God with our efforts. When I get discouraged with my activist work, when it feels like the mountain is too tall to climb, I try to remind myself of all that God has done for me in the past—from baseball to saving my son to leading me to activism. I pray to God a prayer of gratitude daily, "Why me?" For many, this is a victimized prayer as they point the finger at God for the hardships and traumas in their lives. For me, I spin it around. *Why me, God? Why bless me with all these opportunities? Why save me? Why use me in this way to help heal your world?*

In Joshua 2:1, it appears that Joshua had been promoted to scouting director. Rahab received two scouts that Joshua sent as spies, saying to them, "Go, look over the land, especially Jericho." In Joshua 18, the scouts "wrote its description on a scroll, town by town, in seven parts, and returned to Joshua in the camp at Shiloh."

Of course, the battle of Jericho would become momentous in the Israelites' journey to the Promised Land. Joshua's skills as a scout and now as a scouting director ultimately led to victory as he completed the work that Moses began.

When we scout the enemy, we too will be victorious.

Spiritual Darkness

On Moses's journey into his leadership position, his upbringing gave him a deep knowledge of the Egyptian culture and the inner workings of Egypt's most powerful people. Moses was a scout without realizing it. He gained useful wisdom about the ways and mindsets of Egyptian oppressors simply because he was on the inside. Moses was a unique person to lead the Hebrew people because of his vast knowledge of the "enemy." We can also probably assume that Moses, though perhaps disgusted by Pharaoh's generational ill-treatment of the Hebrew people, may not have even seen Pharaoh and the Egyptians as enemies. How could he? They rescued, raised, nurtured, and probably loved him.

I invite you to take this same posture when "scouting the enemy" in your fight against injustice. You need to understand what you're going up against. You might need to gain a deep understanding of the mindset of those you believe to be oppressors. Like Moses, consider becoming embedded in a different culture to understand their fears and insecurities and gain a certain kind of compassion for them. Moses eventually learned to seek *restorative* justice.

Remember, the Egyptians *also* suffered from the enslavement of the Israelites because, in their dehumanization of others they found inferior, they became less human themselves. In scouting the enemy, we want to understand the complexities of the darkness we come up against, but we don't want to "get even." Notice that the Israelites' goal was not to fight and kill the Egyptians so that they could take over their kingdom and enslave *them*. They simply no longer wanted to be slaves.

When I use the word "enemy" in this book, you can probably tell by now that what I mean most often is spiritual darkness. As we scout the enemy, let's seek *freedom*, not retribution, an understanding of the darkness we face rather than project our own darkness back onto the enemy. Tearing down another person or taking part in publicly humiliating someone are often efforts to make oneself look good or virtue signal to a particular crowd. This is the opposite of justice. I call it faux justice.

Like Moses, let's take what we've learned and let it embolden our mission. For us, education *is* prevention. Scouting the enemy in the trafficking fight involves going after buyers, traffickers, the culture of objectification, and the loopholes in our legal system.

Scouting Buyers

In our intervention work, we attempt to go after the buyers' reputations. Buyers might not be worried that they will get in legal trouble, but if we can interfere with the messages they send via the Internet, we can threaten to expose what they're doing to their families, friends, employers, and local authorities. They might think that the power and influence they gained in their life has made them invincible—free from reproach—but that's exactly one way we attack when we intervene.

Because of the less-than-severe punishments in our legal system, we have to work extra hard at the USIAHT to impact demand. It's dark, disturbing, and not for the faint of heart. We go out on the street. We receive tips and share that information with law enforcement. We get plugged into specific neighborhoods where trafficking unfolds in the shadows. We take the information we gather—through conversations we have with people on the street and with our technology—and use what we've collected to equip law enforcement, social workers, and rescue teams. We work directly with hackers and cyber security, always looking for creative technology that can prevent and rescue children from the hell they are in.

When we take all the information we've gathered to law enforcement, we are absolutely sure we are targeting the right person. We have to give law enforcement the best information we can so that they are within their rights to go in and hopefully make an arrest. Sometimes, law enforcement isn't interested in certain battles and, therefore, doesn't respond to the information. This is truly frustrating. Because of the challenges in winning a case, District Attorneys and Prosecutors often won't prosecute the traffickers and buyers. Some states have laws on the books where they could actually do something. But, say, law enforcement does get involved. Sometimes, the District Attorneys and Prosecutors drop the ball.

Sometimes, we have to work "around" law enforcement because of their hesitancy to act. Often times when we gain information, I pass the information on to a rescue organization like the Association for the Recovery of Children (ARC), whose rescue teams are comprised mostly of former military men and women. It is not uncommon for organizations like these to partner with law enforcement.

I once got a call from a mother in Utah. I have no idea how she got my number. "Can you help me?" she asked desperately. "I think my daughter is being trafficked in Los Angeles."

I got her daughter's name, background, and some photos—and passed the information to the ARC. Between our technology and their technology (which is only getting more detailed with the developments of AI), the ARC was able to definitively discover that she was being trafficked in Venice, California. And we found her and got her back to her family.

Scouting Traffickers

Along with going after buyers, we also utilize an initiative called Project Reachout where our technology can scrape the phone numbers of the victims being trafficked online. Through Project Reachout, we connect with 1,000-plus victims every month. We send out hundreds of texts a week to these numbers, making them aware that we know about their situation. We ask them if they want out, let them know what they can do to get out, and see if they need our help. We have 30,000 victims—women, girls, and boys—in Tampa, Florida, alone—that this text goes out to. Our goal is to implement this technology in other major trafficking cities around the country.

All the data we gather—as horrific as it is to confront, for this is truly some of the darkest minds on the planet—help us to understand the mindsets of traffickers better. If we can more easily see who they are trying to target, then we can identify trends and target them. If we can see what situations they are trying to exploit, then we can intercept and disrupt them—we can exploit *their* weaknesses.

For example, recent data shows that sixty to seventy percent of all trafficked kids are coming out of foster care. A staggering eighty-eight percent of *runaway*—whom traffickers groom and sell for sex—are involved with the foster care system. Why? Foster children are some of the most vulnerable kids in society. They are accustomed to moving from home to home, so they crave stability. Traffickers exploit that need.

In the grooming process, traffickers will provide kids with clothes, food, and other luxuries, fooling the kids into thinking they have finally found safety and love. Pimps intentionally strive to meet a deep subconscious need in the lives of these young people. They are incredibly manipulative.

We've all heard stories about foster parents who depend upon having foster children for their income and might not care about the formative hearts and minds of the children they're hosting. Kids pick up on this. Some theorize that children can become used to attaching their worth to a paycheck. Suddenly, a foster parent's commodification of a child serves as a psychological onramp for a trafficker to do the same. Recent studies have also shown that there has been an increase in disabled children being sex trafficked. Traffickers and buyers really do prey on vulnerability. They see these precious children made in the image of God as "other" and make their living dehumanizing them. Yes, I get angry. And so should you. Do something.

My friend and fellow anti-trafficking warrior in Las Vegas, Jack Martin—the former director at the Clark County Department of Juvenile Justice Services—has seen firsthand the horrors of the child welfare and foster care systems. The welfare system investigates abusive situations, while the foster care system is supposed to place children with foster families. Jack entered the child welfare system at two days old when it was discovered that his biological father had abused him, resulting in two broken arms and a fractured skull. In the early seventies, the child welfare system was not equipped to communicate across jurisdictions, so anytime he was located, the family would move. Jack lived in eight different states before he was eight years old.

Eventually landing in Los Angeles, California, his biological parents abandoned him once and for all, landing him permanently in foster care, where he went in and out of juvenile detention facilities for his inability to manage his violent behaviors. One can understand why. Sadly, his situation did not improve in foster care. One family made him eat dog food. Another set up fights between him and the other foster kids as the foster parents sat around and watched. Another forced his foster children to work at his store every day when they were supposed to be at school. Another family made the foster children perform nonstop chores around the house while their biological kids made fun of them. The list goes on.

Jack was eventually embraced by who he now considers his parents, Raul and Mercedes, undocumented citizens raising twelve of their own children. These two wonderful people introduced him to the beauties of Mexican culture and invited him to become a part of their expansive family. After graduating high school from inside a juvenile camp and losing a brother to gang violence, Jack changed his mindset and attitude. He pursued a career in corrections that eventually led to his current position as a probation officer in Southern Nevada. He's continuing the legacy of Raul and Mercedes: using the challenges in his life to connect and uplift others. Blessed to have been saved from a life of violence, Jack remains committed to reforming the child welfare and foster care systems as he impacts children to find their hope and learn to dream again.

We've also found in our "scouting" that most trafficked kids are minorities, particularly in big cities. They are predominately blacks, Hispanics, and people from the LGBTQ community. In Los Angeles, we're finding that almost ninety percent of trafficked minors are people of color. In Las Vegas, it's estimated that seventy-two percent of trafficked children are African-American girls. In Florida, the estimate is that over ninety percent of trafficked children are minorities. When profit calls the shots, the boulder is typically already rolling down the hill. Standing in the way of a tumbling rock and trying to stop it is a good way to get squashed or seriously hurt. Still, it's a challenge I'm willing to face.

For example, in Las Vegas, where it's advertised that all sin is permissible, a tourist may slip the concierge a hundred-dollar bill and wink, "I'm looking for a younger person." The concierge then gets kickback from the trafficker. Sometimes, the tourists engaging in this behavior are also the casino's biggest gamblers. So, to crack down heavily on trafficking and prostitution would not only hurt the "anything goes" branding of Vegas but would also lead to fewer wealthy people dropping tens of thousands in Vegas for a weekend getaway.

Scouting Culture

I'm sure you've heard the famous adage "sex sells." Conditioned in our society to tolerate unhealthy sexual expression in our culture, it's no wonder that only fifty-five percent of adults twenty-five and over (researched by Covenant Eyes) believe that pornography is wrong. As I've mentioned, this is often directly tied to trafficking.

But this is not *just* a problem that everyone in our society should fight. Think about tech companies and advertisers that profit off of pornography. Think about some of our largest media networks that serve as onramps to porn use or trafficking with programming that cheapens sex.

Pornography is a $97 billion global industry ($12 billion in the United States alone), which often serves as a gateway to trafficking. An organization called Covenant Eyes projects that by 2025, VR porn will be a $1 billion industry. The popularity of pornography epitomizes the rampant dehumanization and objectification in our country, and it is slowly tarnishing one of the most sacred elements of what being human means: sex.

Our hyper-sexualized culture has a way of desensitizing your mind and cheapening sexual expression. Recent feminist movements have even tried to frame sex work as bold and empowering. What impact might this have on young girls? Might men then use this to justify their actions?

Scouting Systems

We got a rude awakening regarding the nature of politics when, in 2018 under the direction and encouragement of the Florida government, we opened Hero House, our safe home for boys. The Department of Children and Family Services told us the state was overrun with boys they had rescued from being trafficked and that there was a big need for a safe home that provided trauma-informed care. So, we opened a spacious, comfortable home in a mysterious location that could house five to six boys at a time. It seemed like a great partnership.

However, that department failed to fill our home for the next four years, always giving us a new excuse despite their *own* annual trafficking report plateauing at 80-90 rescued boys per year. Their numbers had not decreased, but our safe home often remained occupied too often by only two or three boys at a time. If that story I shared about yelling at the Florida governor's advisor got you curious about the context, this was it. It was as if there was a complete breakdown in getting these kids who had been through hell the trauma care they needed.

When we would call Florida DCF or even the attorney general's office to figure out what was going on, we were once told that our human trafficking report numbers were incorrect and that the problem wasn't as big as we were making it out to be.

"Those are your numbers we're quoting," we said plainly.

They sure did love telling Florida voters and donors that the state had the only designated safe home in the country for trafficked boys, though—politics at its finest.

When you look at some of these organizations and government initiatives, one can't help but wonder, "Do they really want to solve the problem they claim they are helping? Or, is their goal to keep their ministry or nonprofit running?" Homelessness in San Francisco is a good example of this. If you're serving more homeless people every year, that doesn't necessarily mean that what you're doing is working. You should serve *fewer* homeless people every year if you're genuinely rehabilitating people and reacclimatizing them into society. Our goal at USIAHT is to work ourselves out of a job. Hopefully, this book will be no longer relevant in a couple of years.

We learned a hard lesson in that experience with our safe home for trafficked boys. If we wanted to make a dent in this fight, we needed to make an impact from the inside out. We needed to find a way to infiltrate the system.

This, however, would turn out to be even more daunting.

To give you a glimpse of how broken our legal system concerning trafficking, the punishment in most places in the United States for paying to have sex with a child is a minor fine and a slap on the wrist. And that's if it's ever prosecuted. Why? The biggest legal issue is that there usually isn't enough proof to charge someone. What child will know to go to the authorities immediately after an assault so that a rape kit can be employed? And, on top of that, how are they supposed to escape the abuse and manipulation of the trafficker who is enslaving them? As I've mentioned, boys are especially guarded when seeking help or sharing their stories.

All of these systemic dynamics of trafficking are why we felt the need to make our case at state capitols, and in Washington, D.C. There needs to be more severe legal punishment for traffickers, buyers, and possessors of child pornography. Our foster care system needs to be reformed. We need to have a serious conversation in this country about the psychological impacts of pornography. We need to financially cripple the booming trafficking industry so that there are no financial incentives. One of the most effective ways to change demand is to create harsher trafficking laws. You better believe that if someone is messed up enough in the head to rape a child for money, they're probably more than willing to risk the consequences of paying a minor fine. We're determined to change this, one city at a time.

Sometimes, I can't help but wonder: Have we turned a blind eye to the children in our country? This is evident in the six-billion-dollar human trafficking industry and in how politicians haven't prioritized lawmaking that could help stop this situation. Prosecutors and District Attorneys often fail to enforce the laws currently on the books. Why? Big tech targets children with manipulative algorithms, damaging their brains for profit's sake. Social media companies *could* crack down on the child sex trafficking that takes place on their platforms but haven't made it a top priority. We are grateful for one state Attorney General who recently called out Mark Zuckerberg, whom she felt had some culpability for the problem because of what he allowed to exist on his platform. Facebook, TikTok, and Instagram are often where buyers lurk to find trafficked children. Politicians standing up to

Big Tech will be an important part of this fight.

When people ask me why I'm so passionate about putting an end to human trafficking, I simply point them to Jesus. Jesus's tender heart for children in Matthew 18 is followed up with a cold warning to those who don't care for children. I hope you take stern warnings seriously as this chapter ends: "If anyone causes one of these little ones—those who believe in me—to stumble, it would be better for them to have a large millstone hung around their neck and to be drowned in the depths of the sea. Woe to the world because of the things that cause people to stumble! Such things must come, but woe to the person through whom they come!"

In the summer of 2019, we learned about a nine-year-old child in Missouri who was trafficked since he was four. He and his mother were trafficked by her husband, his biological father. For years, she and her son were moved from county, region, and state without the mother remembering anything because her "husband" kept her continuously drugged. She would "fall asleep" in one state and wake up in another. How could something like this happen for so long? I was recently talking to a data analyst for the Las Vegas Metro PD criminal intelligence department who was sharing with me that they have discovered numerous networks of traffickers who communicate with one another in unregulated, secretive chatrooms on the dark web, and some not. Again, this is another reason why Big Tech needs to get more involved in this fight. This man was able to make lots of money selling his *own* family in different regions around the country, likely because of this underground network, *and* avoid being caught because he was constantly "on the run."

It wasn't until the boy was nine years old that the case was discovered, and the mother began seeking help. She reached out to local services in Missouri, desperately seeking a safe place for her son. The child was violent toward his mother because he viewed her as the reason he was being trafficked. He did not blame the trafficker but blamed his mother. This is why there is a need for trauma-informed care and safe homes.

The child was referred to Hero House, yet the Missouri Department of Social Services (Children's Division) couldn't get through the hurdle of government bureaucracy to fund his recovery. And neither could Florida's Department of Child and Family Services because this child was not a Florida resident. Think about that for a second. This child, trafficked from state to state for five straight years by a sick man, couldn't receive necessary trauma-informed care because of something as unimportant as his residency. The truth is, he had no residency.

And we never got the chance to help him.

15
STANDING IN THE GAP

"For while we may not be able to make the difference for all, we can make all the difference for one."
~Gary A. Haugen

Post MLB baseball, an opportunity opened up for me to own a Mercedes Benz dealership in Santa Clarita, California. I knew little about cars—I could barely put gas in one. But one of my good friends, an Orthodox Jew named Sam Eltes, a part owner of the Expos while I was the General Manager, owned a Benz dealership and introduced me to a special opportunity north of Los Angeles. He introduced me to Mercedes Benz corporate, and the rest was up to me to make it happen. Not only did it seem like a good investment, but the gig would also allow me to have a flexible schedule, which was important to be a more present father and invest more of my time into ministry and mission trips. It was a unique and random opportunity, something I never saw myself doing, but I couldn't help but feel like it was a good fit. I agreed to build and open a brand-new Benz dealership.

Much to my surprise, I *really* enjoyed it. For many people, buying a Benz is a lifelong dream, and I loved seeing hardworking, everyday people's faces light up when they could finally make that dream a reality at our dealership. In my other two places of employment after the Dodgers—at the Master's College and the Los Angeles Dream Center—I served in more of a fundraising capacity (which was more like "friend-raising") and enjoyed both roles. At the dealership, it was nice to be back in a leadership position: overseeing a team, creating culture, elevating integrity in an industry where greed often reigns, and having a positive impact on the local community through our philanthropic wing. I still didn't know much about cars, but I could use my gifts as a relationship-builder and networker to serve.

However, a couple of years into the dealership I began to sense that something was off. Unfortunately, I am legally bound to be vague here, but I'll try to be as transparent as possible. I noticed that the dealership culture wasn't living up to the reputation I had set before our team. Something seemed to be transpiring in the shadows that was undercutting everything we had built as a team and as a culture. I began to suspect that some elaborate illegal activities were happening. When all was said and done, it cost my family and me approximately $5 million to $10 million.

I've never been about money, though. For me, baseball was about championships, not the bottom line. What annoyed me most about this circumstance was how everything we built had been tarnished—as a team, as a culture—and how the transgressions directly affected my hardworking employees. We really had something special happening at that dealership.

During that time, I went to a dark place. Since being taken advantage of by those priests in my youth, I never had much patience for bullies. I never had much patience for people who thought they were above accountability.

Most frustrating was that the justice I craved was impossible to pursue or, at least would have taken years of financial commitment. I felt stuck. Handcuffed.

Upon reflection, I wonder if I felt "triggered" by these actions because of its parallels with the priests in my youth. There is a reason sexual abuse was rampant within the Catholic Church in many American communities for so long. Those priests felt protected by the systems around them. We've since learned that in many communities, the local archdiocese was also in cahoots with law enforcement and the local judicial system. Those priests who preyed upon children felt they could get away with anything. And in our community, they did—for a long time.

When it came to these heartbreaking challenges that negatively impacted our dealership—putting people I cared for in an awful financial and professional predicament—my heart became hijacked by an all-consuming rage. If the systems being hid behind were too difficult to break through for justice to be served, then maybe I needed to act upon the injustice myself. I admit that I was so angry that it blurred my morals. Have you ever been there?

One Sunday morning, Marilyn and I were at church, and the sermon couldn't have been more timely. The message was about struggling to forgive. The next day, I made the hardest phone call I've ever made, asking for forgiveness for *my* dark thoughts. "I've been having some really dark thoughts about you," I said, "and I just wanted to call you and ask you for forgiveness." Counterintuitive as it was, I realized that I needed to search my heart and eradicate the darkness. Experiencing betrayal by friends and family is hard to overcome.

I can't help but think that this situation helped prepare me for activism. Scouting the enemy, as you've found in this book, is twofold: one that is both systemic and personal. A darkness pervades this world through selfish people and flawed systems. This all conflates to form an evil force that tears through communities and ruins lives. Paul warns us about this in Ephesians 6:12, "For our struggle is not against flesh and blood, but against the rulers, against the authorities, against the powers of this dark world and against the spiritual forces of evil in the heavenly realms."

You don't need me telling you how dark the world is. If you've been engaged in your justice fight for a while now, you know.

Standing in the gap in the face of this darkness can be intimidating. It can be complex. It can sometimes feel overwhelming. Many activists experience burnout—feeling like they are spinning their wheels but going nowhere—as they face seemingly unchangeable systems. Sometimes, change can feel as slow as getting a cargo ship to change directions.

Yet, it's not only about scouting the authorities and powers of this dark world, but also about how some of that same darkness might sometimes infiltrate our own lives. That's why continually being introspective and gauging your own heart, mind, and personal well-being is important in activism. As a Christian, I could not do this without my prayer life: constantly bowing before the throne and surrendering to Him my fears, angst, and the darkness that has found its way into my heart. One of my "life songs" is Phil Wickham's "Battle Belongs"—he sings that the crux of our fights happens on our knees.

Darkness is complex. Genesis 3:1 reveals that the serpent that tricked Adam and Even was "more crafty than any of the wild animals." As John 10:10 tells us, "the thief comes only to steal and kill and destroy," but Jesus has come so that we "may have life, and have it to the full." Activists, in my experience, might be even more at risk of being enveloped by the darkness of this world. We have had key employees at USIAHT feel the need to resign because of the weight of the darkness. That's because scouting the enemy requires getting frighteningly *close* in order to understand its ways.

Taking on the Darkness

God called Moses to stand in the gap, shine the spotlight on evil, and make Pharaoh and the Egyptian elite accountable for not honoring human dignity in their enslavement and mistreatment of the Israelites. God called Moses to *name* the evil and offer Pharaoh a redemptive path forward. If Pharaoh didn't obey, God promised that He would act himself.

After much protest toward Yahweh and His call, Moses eventually submitted. He told Jethro he was going to return to Egypt and receive his blessing (Exodus 4:18). He met with Aaron (Exodus 4:27-18), an Israelite, who would become an essential justice partner for Moses as they sought to liberate the Israelites. They met with the Israelite elders, and Aaron justified the call Moses had heard from Yahweh (Exodus 4:29-31), as the two of them received the elders' blessing. After fleeing Egypt, after decades in Midian, after all his protesting of Yahweh's call, Moses's mission was now, finally, in motion. He was going deeper into the plot of his life, God's plan for him, and his justice-rooted purpose.

He would quickly learn, however, just how complicated it would be to stand in the gap. After Moses proclaimed to Pharaoh to "let my people go," Pharaoh increased his persecution of the Israelites by severely increasing their workload. The pain of the Israelite slaves from their increase in labor led the Israelite overseers to complain to Moses and Aaron. "May the Lord look on you and judge you!" they said. "You have made us obnoxious to Pharaoh and his officials and have put a sword in their hand to kill us" (Exodus 5:19-21).

One can imagine how excruciating this had to have been. Moses's actions, which God called him to do, led to *more* pain for the Israelites he was trying to liberate. His actions caused them to distrust him *more*, though he needed their trust to lead them out of slavery. Activism is a dizzying experience! Instead of getting angry at Pharaoh, they got angry at him! As Moses stood in the gap between God and the Israelites, and between the Egyptians and the Israelites. His people's doubt and anger toward *him* created doubt and anger toward *God* within him. At the end of the fifth chapter, Moses cried out to God, "Why, Lord, why have you brought trouble on this people? Is this why you sent me? Ever since I went to Pharaoh to speak in your name, he has brought trouble on this people, and you have not rescued your people at all" (5:22-23).

Moses didn't realize it at the time, but this complexity in the gap would become his reality all the way to the Promised Land.

He stood in the gap between the Israelites and God, between their doubt/frustration and God's direction. Moses bore the weight of it all. The Israelites' suffering. Their complaints. God's call. His frustration with them, with *him*. Through it all, Moses never stopped having an intimate relationship with God. He spoke to God freely, honestly, and openly. This is a lesson in itself—no matter how frustrated or confused Moses became as he stood in the gap between Yahweh and the Israelites, he never quit the mission. He kept going. He kept fighting. He kept praying and talking to God, even if those conversations were difficult.

Not For Sale

The Bible uses the phrase "stand in the gap" only once—in Ezekiel 22:30, "I looked for someone among them who would build up the wall and stand before me in the gap on behalf of the land so I would not have to destroy it, but I found no one." In my opinion, this phrase describes not only the role of Old Testament prophets like Moses and Ezekiel but also Jesus's ministry. Jesus stood in the gap between us and God, between sin and perfect holiness, and reunited us with our Creator. Standing in the gap, Jesus took the fullness of sin and darkness upon himself and died on the cross.

As we pursue our justice-centered purpose to make this world a better place, we will have to "stand in the gap." Between darkness and light. Between perpetrators and victims. Between systems and people. And, as I've found out way too many times with my fiery personality, between stimulus and response. In the anti-trafficking fight, standing in the gap on a local level is absolutely vital for activists.

In 2022, we launched Kids Not For Sale (kidsnotforsale.org), a community-based initiative that fights human trafficking primarily in Las Vegas. It's similar to the USIAHT but different in its local focus and mission. Just as the USIAHT has been nationally recognized as a premier not-for-profit organization committed to ending human trafficking in the United States, Kids Not for Sale's goal is to address this problem with a more local and regional focus.

Eighty to ninety percent of human trafficking organizations focus on victim services. This is great; these children *need* restoration. But who is going to fight demand? Who will interfere before a trafficker or buyer destroys a child for life? Our dream would be for every major city or state to have its own Kids Not for Sale initiative that strategically attacks human trafficking in that particular area.

Southern Nevada faces unique challenges. Las Vegas is in the top thirteen high-intensity child trafficking areas in the United States. When children are caught being forced to solicit sex, Nevada's default response (like most states in our country) is to prosecute rather than help. The sex trade is also tied up in the culture of Las Vegas, and here's why:

1. Much of Southern Nevada's economy stems from the lure of overt sexual stimulation, particularly in places like Las Vegas, unfortunately known as "Sin City."
2. The culture of indulgence and anonymity that Nevada incites fosters the economic "demand" for purchased sex.
3. Such a culture of anonymity has spawned legislative, educational, and community apathy, which has made it possible for traffickers to groom and exploit minors to sell for sex. Most Clark County influencers and power brokers talk a good game about how they'll fight child sex trafficking, but it's only talk. None of them take any action that will truly help protect kids. I'm hoping I'll be surprised and that this status quo will change.
4. This perpetual child exploitation "hub" is infiltrating the rest of the United States, continuing to destroy the lives of children, women, and even men.

We started Kids Not For Sale—and we intend to launch KNFS in other cities around the country—because we realized at the USIAHT that certain areas needed a regional response and strategy that met their direct needs. Usually, the biggest challenge to doing this is having resources. The money necessary to make a big difference is nowhere to be found. People naturally grow uncomfortable confronting the reality of human trafficking and sometimes (even subconsciously) prefer to remain on the sidelines. We *believe* and *hope* a significant transformation can happen in Las Vegas and throughout the United States.

We need a more targeted approach for "standing in the gap."

Divine Intervention

A common theme throughout the entire Bible is divine intervention. God often intervenes, it seems, through *people*—through Moses as he led the Israelites out of captivity, through the prophets as they tried to bring healing to God's chosen people, through Jesus when he was born as a humble baby to lead a sinless life and suffer a death that rescued us all, through the apostles as they sought to follow Jesus's teachings and spread his loving message to all.

Time and time again throughout the Bible, God works through flawed people to accomplish His purposes—to bring love and healing to a hurting world. I like to think of activism in this same light. We can partner with God and allow Him to work through us as we intervene—as we stand in the gap—for His healing purposes. Sometimes, Christians think that because God's work culminated in Jesus Christ, His work in the world ended on the cross. This couldn't be further from the truth. The Holy Spirit lives in me and you. He works in and through us, sanctifying us and animating our hands and feet as we work in the world.

Jesus speaks of this in John 14, "I will not leave you as orphans; I will come to you. Before long, the world will not see me anymore, but you will see me. Because I live, you also will live. On that day you will realize that I am in my Father, and you are in me, and I am in you."

How do we let the Holy Spirit work through us? We have to be formed by the Word of God and grow in our relationship with Him. Activism is such an intense calling—sometimes overwhelming as we confront the full weight of inept (and corrupt) systems—that the only solution is to do everything possible to be healthy and centered internally. Awareness is and should include a call to action. Intervention *is* action.

The prophets were activists. Jesus, as we've mentioned, was an activist. They all had to sift through internal and external noise to intercede for those they came to serve. Think about the intensity of Jesus's emotions in the Garden of Gethsemane. Think about the sense of abandonment Jesus felt on the cross when he cried out, "My God, why have you forsaken me?" Consider the scrutiny he faced from the religious elite of that day and the betrayal he experienced from his closest friends. Standing in the gap is not for the faint of heart.

At times, you might feel caught in a web of conflicting voices. You might feel stuck in a mental or emotional spiral. You might, like Moses, face anger and complaints from the very people you're trying to serve. I love that phrase—*stand in the gap*—because it captures the complexity of our call as seekers of justice.

Our world is very noisy, and sometimes, it's difficult to decipher what is true. I encourage you to do what Moses did and take all your emotions, doubts, and frustrations to God. God is big enough to handle the complexity you carry and *wants* you to take your troubles to Him. As 1 Peter 5:7 says, "Cast all your anxiety on Him because He cares for you."

This world can be intense, but we have a God who willingly entered into *our* suffering and stood in the gap for us.

16
LET MY PEOPLE GO!

"What we do in life echoes in eternity."
~Marcus Aurelius

In the spring of 1995, in the middle of the MLB strike, we (like every team) called and signed a bunch of washed-up backups (no offense to them) to fill our Montreal roster during spring training. We were getting guys who hadn't played baseball in years. One was a former player driving a beer truck during the week and playing softball on Sundays. "Yeah, I can play!" he exclaimed, all fired up.

One day, during a press conference, a reporter asked me, "What do you think about Donald Fehr?" He was the Executive Director for the MLB Player Association, one of the most powerful men in baseball during the 1994 strike. In my mind, he was also one of the key figures who prevented our Montreal team from making a run at the World Series the year before since the season came to a screeching halt, the first time since 1904 (nearly a century!) that didn't have a World Series. Fans were also quickly losing interest in baseball, disgusted that there was a squabble with how much money both owners and players were making. It would take years to recover, and then MLB took another blow with the Steroid Era.

Without hesitation, I responded to the reporter, "Every time I see his face, I want to puke."

All MLB executives were mad at him; in my mind, I had spoken for all of them. I figured the interview might show up in a little French-Canadian outlet.

When Marilyn and I were relaxing on the couch that evening and watching ESPN, we heard the iconic *SportsCenter* theme—"DaDaDa! DaDaDa!"—and then—*BOOM!*—my face popped onto the screen.

Marilyn looked over at me and said, "What'd you do now?"

You become pretty familiar with that question after nearly three decades of marriage.

And believe me, she has gotten used to asking it.

"I don't know what I did," I told her.

She buried her head in her hands.

When they got to the segment, I shrugged and said, "Somebody needed to say it."

"Okay," Marilyn said, "but why is it always you?"

Donald Fehr and I had a good phone conversation after my comments and became friends. He said, "If I were you, I'd probably say the same thing."

The strike settled, and I focused my sights on trying to help get Montreal to the playoffs despite the fire-sell of all our stars the year before: John Wetteland, Marquis Grissom, Kenny Hill, and Larry Walker. We were competitive—showing flashes of brilliance—but our inexperience showed. As we neared the trade deadline, I knew we needed some experience and began to make a move for veteran first baseman and switch-hitter David Segui. The New York Mets agreed to the trade, but it would entail Montreal paying out Segui's contract of $800,000 for the second half of the season. In case you don't follow baseball, that's not very much money in the grand scheme of things. However, every slightest extension of the budget *is* a big deal when you're the General Manager of a team with one of the MLB's smallest payrolls.

Claude Brochu, the part-owner and President of the Expos, always supported my baseball moves and decisions but was hesitant to pull the trigger on the trade. As we got into crunch time, I pressured him, "What are we going to do? How can we compete with a team like the Braves or Yankees if we can't make moves like this?"

"I don't think we can do it," he responded.

I called a couple of other executives—they told me the same thing, "Don't do it."

Well, I did it.

After all, you can cut the fat off the meat, but if you keep cutting, you eventually start cutting into the bone. I had to do what was best for the team. But I knew then and there that the writing was on the wall regarding my time in Montreal.

I got another one of those looks from Marilyn that said, "What is wrong with you?"

I wouldn't shut up as an MLB General Manager. The truth needs to be said. And I'm not shutting up now. In our culture, we're angry, mad, and upset about everything under the sun, so why are we, as Americans, not upset—not *outraged*—at the sex slavery of our boys and girls?

Imago Dei

Jesus had a tender heart for children, even though they (along with women) had minimal social standing in the culture of his day. Yet Jesus himself came to this world through a willing, holy woman and was born as a baby. Think about that. The incarnation hinges upon these two most neglected (and abused) demographics of their day. This is the God of justice we worship and trust—a God who truly cares about his sons and daughters—*His* children—being treated as if they are the *imago dei*, made in His image.

Luke 18 has a scene where people brought their babies to Jesus so he could place his hands on them and bless them. Jesus's disciples, believing that the Lord had better things to do, rebuked the families for wasting Jesus's time. Jesus stopped the disciples from what they were doing and said, "Let the little children come to me, and do not hinder them, for the kingdom of God belongs to such as these. Truly I tell you, anyone who will not receive the kingdom of God like a little child will never enter it."

We witness a similar scene in Matthew 18. When his disciples—caught up in comparing and stuck in their hierarchical approach to religion—asked him who was the greatest in the kingdom of heaven, Jesus called a small child to him and placed the child among the disciples, perhaps lifting the child onto his lap. Jesus then said, "Truly I tell you, unless you change and become like little children, you will never enter the kingdom of heaven. Therefore, whoever takes the lowly position of this child is the greatest in the kingdom of heaven. And whoever welcomes one such child in my name welcomes me."

Those who witnessed the scene would have been shocked. To say that a *child* is the greatest in the kingdom of heaven was to flip religion on its head. Judaism at that time mainly had become influenced by self-righteousness and legalism, as we see in Jesus's exchanges with the Pharisees and Sadducees. This top-down hierarchical approach to religion likely infiltrated the minds of Jesus's disciples as well. Their very question indicates that they were also comparing and ranking who was the greatest in the kingdom.

This brings us back to Moses. When Moses was born, Pharaoh had just issued the order for the massacre of every Hebrew newborn male to limit the growth of the Hebrew race. Isn't it interesting that, despite this decree, Pharaoh's daughter could not resist adopting Moses as her own when she first opened that basket on the Nile River and saw his face? It was as if she knew, deep down, that she was encountering the Imago Dei, though she wouldn't have used that language. Her own father's racist decree did not matter; she was going to raise Moses as her own.

We need to take this same stance in the trafficking fight. It's easy to ignore these young people being trafficked in inner cities, run-down factory towns impacted by the opioid crisis, and in foster homes all around the country. We too easily label them as "other," so we don't have to feel that sickening feeling in our hearts. But this is just a defense mechanism. Ignorance is *not* bliss. It simply leads to living a life without purpose.

Whatever issue of injustice God has placed on your heart, it probably has something to do with human dignity. If it doesn't, I'd argue that the calling probably isn't coming from God. As a Christian, I believe every single person is made in the image of God, what is called the *imago dei*. I believe this is the truest thing about us.

In Christianity, this notion of an undeniable connectedness to one another is called the Body of Christ. Paul encourages us in 1 Corinthians 12:21-26 that each person is part of the body and has a vital role. I believe Paul used this metaphor specifically for the burgeoning church of his day—with all their disagreements and conflict as Christianity expanded to include both Jews and Gentiles—but I think it could just as easily apply to all of us as Americans.

The founders of the United States had a similar message when they suggested the motto, "Out of many, one." If we saw ourselves as connected to the body with a role that benefits the whole, we would find no need to objectify or dehumanize one another. Trafficking would not exist because people would realize the boy or girl being marketed or sold is someone's son or daughter, with a spirit, soul, and infinite talents that ought to be cultivated in a healthy environment to make our world a better place. There would be less demand for Internet pornography because people would start seeing those on their screens as living, breathing, beautiful persons rather than objects to be used. Corporate greed, resulting in the dehumanization of workers for the sake of the bottom line, would be less frequent because the health and happiness of employees would become more important or just as necessary as making a profit.

Even if you're not a Christian, it's difficult to deny the rich, healing values within this metaphor of the Body of Christ. The body is also a fitting image because we become more *disembodied* as individuals the more we objectify or dehumanize one another. It's time to become *one* body again, with each of us encouraging and empowering one another to play a meaningful role. Jesus's most important commandment is to love God—and to love others, who are made in His image.

Mary's Story

We once had a kid, born as a male, come through our safe home who identified as a transgender female. This situation is not uncommon in the fight against human trafficking. People who identify as LGBTQ are some of the most vulnerable to trafficking. They are more likely to find themselves on the streets as they face rejection from their loved ones, and traffickers often target them, exploit their vulnerabilities, and use them as a commodity to meet the sexual desires of their customers.

This child, let's call her Mary, sometimes wore a dress. Other times, she wore boy clothes. Sometimes, she talked about wanting to change her name. Other times, she seemed content to be who she was. The staff's goal at the safe home was focused: to address her trauma, not to convince her to identify with the gender she was assigned at birth. It wasn't some form of "conversation" therapy. Our staff never tried to convince a child that they weren't gay or trans. Any human being who has endured the hell these kids have navigated would be sexually confused. Our role was to provide love and care.

Mary was the Imago Dei. And that's all that mattered.

One day, Mary told John, "Hey, I just want you to know that I figured out that this is a Christian organization."

John looked at Mary with a puzzled look, "Okay, does that bother you?

"No," Mary said unconvincingly.

"We're not trying to hide anything," John assured. "We love God, and we love people—*all people*—because that's what Jesus taught us to do."

162

"I've been to church before, and I've been to youth groups," Mary shared. "But they all hated me. They all judged me. And I guess I just expected you guys to be the same."

"No," John said, "we just love you and want you to be safe."

Mary grinned and kind of skipped in her dress out of the room.

Belonging to Each Other

Eight times, Moses told Pharaoh to "Let my people go!" *Eight times.*

Fighting child sex trafficking is more than a one-time event. It takes courage, dedication, determination, endurance, and collaboration for us—all of us—to end human trafficking.

Speaking the truth requires deliberation and grace. I have seen the most success in convincing people to join the human trafficking fight whenever I let them in on my passion rather than my anger, my conviction rather than weaponizing guilt. Interestingly, Moses withheld from demonizing Pharaoh or treating him as a villain. Moses didn't try to attack him. He didn't curse him out. He didn't say, "Pharaoh, you're racist and evil." He simply said, "Let my people go."

Bold. Direct. To the point.

There is something really beautiful about Moses's words, isn't there? God's people became Moses's people. People he had been estranged from most of his life became his brothers and sisters again. He reawakened the conviction he perhaps felt when he killed the Egyptian slave-driver decades before. Despite the Israelites' complaints, he would not abandon his mission. He would not stop loving them, fighting for them. He could not un-see the burning bush or un-hear his call.

The Prodigal Son is one of Jesus's most well-known parables. It's a story about an arrogant son leaving his family, squandering his inheritance with pleasures in a dark world, and returning home after he hit rock bottom. Instead of facing harsh discipline, however, the lost son was embraced by his accepting, loving father and fully welcomed back into the family. Preachers often use this story as a metaphor for our journeys back to God in the emptiness of our sin. I like that interpretation, and it certainly describes my life.

But lately, when I hear this story, I think of the millions of boys and girls *in this very country* who are lost in a dark world by no fault of their own.

They were perhaps born in the wrong place at the wrong time around the wrong people and became lost in a dark, broken world. Children who are trafficked cannot willingly return home, like the prodigal, for they often don't know what home even is, nor can they escape the slavery. My heart breaks to say this, but a "normal life" to many of them *is* abuse, loneliness, and transaction.

Luke 15:20 paints a beautiful scene of God's love for us and how we, too, are to love others: "But while he (the prodigal son) was still a long way off, his father saw him and was filled with compassion for him; he ran to his son, threw his arms around him…" I invite you to echo the father in the parable: to run relentlessly down the path in pursuit of justice, to run *toward* those who are hurting and *fight* for love. See the *Imago Dei* in the person before you. Embrace this daughter or son of God.

17
ROLE-PROFILING

"If you read history you will find that the Christians who did the most for the present world were just those who thought most of the next. It is since Christians have largely ceased to think of the other world that they have become so ineffective in this."
~C. S. Lewis, Mere Christianity

A strategy called "Role Profiling" was one of the reasons why our Minnesota Twins and Montreal Expos teams had so much success despite their fledgling budgets. Role profiling was essentially, say, targeting twenty-five specific roles that you needed on your roster—maybe a leadoff hitter with a high on-base percentage that was also a switch-hitter, or a starting pitcher who could get you two hundred-plus innings a year, or a go-to left-handed pitcher who could cause nightmares for certain left-handed batters, or a versatile shortstop who could also play three or four other positions, or a left-handed-hitting catcher who could play multiple positions. If you knew what roles you were looking for throughout all levels of your organization, you could also communicate the need for these specific roles to your scouts.

Rising through the ranks during the Sabermetrics boom, the temptation for General Managers was to approach decision-making through strict analytics processes. Stats seemed to explain everything, which is even more the case now.

Role Profiling takes a slightly different approach to decision-making—incorporating statistics but not relying on them entirely. Stats and data are essential, but you also want to fulfill specific roles you've identified as crucial to the overall makeup of your team.

That was one of the problems with the Dodgers lineup when I was first hired as a GM. We had a good team statistically. Many players had a decent batting average, and our pitchers had solid ERAs. But we needed more diversity of skill if we were going to be a championship team. Role Profiling forces you to look at the makeup and dynamic within the clubhouse, not just the production profile for each position. The problem these days is that most teams have entire departments dedicated to crunching numbers, but no one in that department knows how to wear a jockstrap and what that means, i.e., how to play the game.

This became a trend for us at almost every organization I worked for. We wanted to take a *deeper* look at our prospects. The research and investigation of a prospect were fundamental to gaining an understanding of the player's personality and character. Was he selfish or selfless? Arrogant or humble? These are vital characteristics of a guy who knows how to win.

I often heard a scout say that a player was a "five-tool guy"— he could hit, power hit, field, run, and throw. Role Profiling even revolutionizes this approach. In scouting, we graded players between 20 (poor) and 80 (outstanding) and went after guys who were two- or three-tool players but were exceptional in those areas. How was a five-tool player who ranked in the 50s in every category going to help us win? Often times we believed in going after someone we rated in the high 60s in a couple of categories if that was a role we needed, even if his rating in the other three categories were in the 40s. We scouted guys who could develop as players and fulfill roles that would help give us an edge.

Role-profiling challenged you as a scout to look deeper than the five-tool approach—to consider how someone could fit on your team, what role he would play, and the strengths he would bring. We discovered that a lot of the five-tool guys were average major league players. But if we had a guy who was a 40 runner but had 60 or 70 power, that tool could help you win games, and the player could be brought in for specific situations.

These days, organizations have entire departments devoted to the science of statistics, and General Managers often call the shots based on statistics alone. I came up at a time when General Managers still trusted scouts' holistic assessments of prospects. That trust has been lost today.

You see this in the 2011 film *Moneyball*—based on Michael Lewis's bestselling book, which caricatures old scouts as clueless, stats-ignoring curmudgeons who are stuck in the ways of the past as they lean on their gut evaluations and personal knowledge for the game. In sports and in fighting injustice, as we've discussed, you need both mind *and* heart. You need to gather information, but you also need your gut instincts. Having a winning makeup is vital—scouts need to look for that. Nothing in life is one-dimensional. To reduce a player to his statistical output might lead to never giving someone a chance who would be a great leader in the clubhouse and could be developed into one of the best catchers in the league (i.e., Mike Piazza). Statistics don't always measure potential.

When I was with the Orioles, we consulted a psychologist who wrote a popular book about brain types based on Myers-Briggs assessments. So, we began incorporating specific brain types into our Role Profiling. We weren't looking for one particular brain type, although some were more desirable than others. We wanted diverse brain types that could fit our team best to create more balance and fill more strengths on the team. The last thing you want when building any team is a bunch of people who think or react the same way. What's important is using all the tools at your disposal to put a winning team on the field.

Through this process, we began to see a mental overlap between shortstops and catchers—positions where players could see or understand all the dynamics of the field in front of them. With a shortage in the league of quality catchers, we began scouting shortstops we thought might have the potential to develop as a catcher. Even crazier, we began to see that guys who played third base and had a great arm might be able to be developed to one day come out of the bullpen.

When people ask me what I miss about baseball, I tell them I miss the diversity of personalities and unique people who make up a clubhouse and organization. Seeing players develop not only as baseball players but as people—as fathers, husbands, and teammates—was one of the great joys of my life.

Role Profiling With Your Team

When Geoff Rogers and I started the USIAHT, we balanced each other perfectly, complementing each other's strengths and covering for each other's lesser strengths. He was a data guy who had a cerebral approach to human trafficking. I was a fiery (yet practical) guy who brought the fullness of my heart into every meeting. He approached everything from a business standpoint while I tried to make sure we were still confronting trafficking head-on with this business-focused strategy. We probably drove each other nuts at times, but we also knew that we complemented one another perfectly and covered one another's blind spots.

Role Profiling didn't stop with us. Our first hire was a prayer warrior. That "job title" is what it sounds like. We wanted prayer to be front and center of our anti-human-trafficking ministry. Because we know we are fighting spiritual warfare.

So, we hired a lady named Chong Henderson, who comes into work and makes a living wage to pray seven to eight hours a day, sometimes more. She prays for every project and every child we're hoping to rescue, for every employee and the challenges they faced that week as they gave their God-given energy to stopping trafficking, for each politician introduced to our cause, for protection, intervention, rescue, and restoration. Chong also prayed for effective meetings, safe travel, and for the USIAHT to receive the necessary financial support.

Praying for that long every day takes a person who is spiritually strong and centered. She knows that she might encounter despair as she brings to God the darkness these children face—as she brings before God some of the most horrific things that take place in this world. I know she experiences all these complicated thoughts and emotions. There is no darker world than child sex trafficking when it comes to scouting the enemy and understanding the mindset of the oppressors—of the traffickers and buyers.

Another example of role profiling is our prevention work. Much of the data mined from our technology as we intercept and disrupt buyers and traffickers is intense. It involves being exposed to myriad websites and images that will wither your mind and shatter your faith in both God and humanity. We realized that, though this work was extremely important, some of the people we hired couldn't handle it. We began hiring people who had the unusual ability to "compartmentalize" the horrors they saw. Like doctors or therapists who could leave the intensity of what they experienced at work when they come home after a long day, we wanted people with emotional equanimity that perhaps at times bordered on being emotionless. Strangely, we needed people who wouldn't get too attached to rescuing the kids they saw on a screen or tracking down a buyer or seller of sex. That kind of detachment was key.

I could never do their job. I would lose my mind. But I'm aware that I have my own role to play on our team. Because of the people around me balancing me out, I can be the guy who goes into meetings with guns blazing. I can be my fiery self, within reason, because that helps move the needle. I'm willing to say what most people won't. Conflict doesn't make me uncomfortable—I thrive in it, sometimes to my own detriment.

A big thing I learned in baseball is the importance of unity. A unified team can overcome all kinds of hurdles: injuries, losing streaks, and scrutiny. In Jesus's famous prayer for unity in John 17, he proclaims that we are all *one* team. Just as he is one with the Father and the Holy Spirit, we are one with each other.

Unity is essential when different nonprofits, NGOs, and churches rally together to fight an epidemic as large and complex as human trafficking. We not only Role Profile the makeup of our teams but also in our networking. One of my passions and priorities in activism is bringing ministries, nonprofits, and NGOs together. Unfortunately, there is not always unity when ministries that serve the same purpose compete with one another for funding. Ministries should not be competitors. They should be partners.

The USIAHT is a hub in which our data-focused, comprehensive approach to fighting human trafficking—combined with our rigorous screening of ministries and organizations—allows us to connect people and organizations to combat a specific problem in a particular area. This will become even more detailed as Kids Not For Sale branches out to other cities and regions.

This is very similar to what I did in baseball when I tried to get our players to focus less on their personal goals and more on team goals. When they focused on making the team better, their careers benefited. You might be shocked by how many churches that won't work together because of differing theological beliefs or how many nonprofits or NGOs won't cooperate because of political ties or bureaucracies that are impossible to break through.

When we act like we are not connected with each other, our house is divided. How can a house divided serve the Lord and heal the world? That doesn't mean that we have to always agree with each other or that we can't have rigorous debate. Families fight. But if organizations, ministries, and opposing political parties can't work together to fight *human trafficking*—one of the most horrific issues of injustice our country faces—how will we lean into our unity in other areas of American life? Let's humble ourselves and live out of our connectedness with each other. And then maybe the world will know that God is love.

Role Profiling the Enemy

I recently got into a heated discussion with a person who was very high up in the Clark County, Nevada, school system. As I advocated for him to adopt our human trafficking curriculum—or any that would work, for that matter—for his schools, he dismissed my proposal as "low priority." No city or county in the country has a booming sex industry like Las Vegas. In fact, they advertise it. Traffickers and groomers prey on children in Clark County all the time—online and in person—and children must be taught to recognize the signs.

A lot of money can be made in human trafficking, especially in Las Vegas.

Children *will* run away from home; let's not forget that reality. Sometimes, that's because of teenage angst, but other times, it is legitimate as they flee an unhealthy or abusive situation. And within forty-eight hours on the street, that child will be approached by a trafficker. All children must know how to see through the manipulative ploys of groomers so that they or their friends don't end up in an even more abusive situation.

However, this bureaucrat in the school system didn't consider the human trafficking curriculum a priority. He was enslaved to politics, unions, and the school board. He was focused on diversity and inclusion but seemed blind to the reality that human trafficking affects black, Hispanic, and LGBTQ children the most. I'm confident in saying that the USIAHT has probably done as much or more for black and LGBTQ youth than most organizations that have formed in recent years to fight for "equity" or "social justice." The human trafficking epidemic affects blacks far more than bad policing; it just doesn't make the headlines or produce viral videos. The human trafficking epidemic affects LGBTQ youth far more than most LGBTQ issues progressives get riled up about in the media.

This is where Role Profiling extends to targeting the enemy as well. In building a championship team, Role Profiling has more to do with skill set and personality, but when targeting the enemy, it works with the data gained from demographic trends like race and class. This is not bias or discrimination—it is simply having a radar for potential buyers and sellers that aligns with the statistics we have about trafficking. For example, the data shows that most buyers are middle- to upper-class white men. Consider someone like Jeffrey Epstein and the people he was taking to his island as extreme examples. Those people had it all and made more money than you and I can begin to fathom. So, why did they feel entitled to exploit the bodies of teenage girls?

I have a theory. Studies have shown that white men account for nearly 70% of suicides in the United States. White men are also historically the most affluent demographic in our country. I believe a spiritual crisis is unfolding beneath the surface. They've tasted the American Dream and found it to be empty. Or, their identity is wrapped up in making money, and now they are arrogant enough to believe they can do whatever they want. The National Center for Health Statistics shows that only one in four men who report intense anxiety or depression daily have spoken to a mental health professional. This creates even more of a sense of isolation. White men are perhaps most likely to be sexually broken and perverse.

Are you beginning to see how statistics and Role Profiling might direct us toward underlying issues? Or, let's say we scrape the data of a buyer whose identity is meticulously hidden and whose communication seems educated or psychologically manipulative. We can make an informed determination that this is a middle- or upper-class person, probably a white male. We can threaten to expose his secrets to his workplace and colleagues where he may be viewed as successful, to his wife and family, and to his community where he has curated his faith-and-family image. We always offer a path for redemption to buyers whose data we've obtained and give them resources to get help. Extreme problems require extreme measures. As much as I may want to hunt down a buyer personally, I know that redemption for them is the ultimate form of justice.

Race and class are undoubtedly at play in human trafficking. Human trafficking seems to be the area in America in which racism thrives the most. Something is happening beneath the surface there, as white middle- and upper-class men rent the bodies of minority children. The fight against racism in this country is so often misdirected. Actual slavery exists in the shadows and haunts our beloved African-American, Hispanic, and LGBTQ children.

Moses: A Covenant Restorer

Does God Role Profile with us? I think He does. I believe He hand-selects willing people to do His work of healing on earth. That's what happened in the story of Moses. Moses may have faced doubts and insecurities but did not turn away from the burning bush. He said to Yahweh, "Here I am." Though he wrestled with God continuously in his leadership journey, he proverbially returned to those three words repeatedly: *Here I am.* Because of Moses's willingness to listen to and partner with God, to continually be led into the unknown, God used Moses to restore His covenant with the Israelites. This humble, unassuming man who fled Egypt would become the chief mediator between Yahweh and the Jewish people.

God is a restorer; therefore, in partnering with God, we must be restorers. In seeking restoration, we align ourselves with the arc of the Bible and God's guiding hand throughout history. Free will has not gone away. As long as there are humans, they will do despicable and disturbing things. But just as God did not give up hope on us, we must not give up on restoration.

Have you ever thought about viewing your activism through a covenantal lens? A covenant is an unbreakable commitment. What are you committed to changing? How can you use your God-given gifts to help heal the world? Again, Moses was an imperfect leader. He had fears. He had doubts. He had an ego. Ultimately, he wasn't granted the privilege of guiding the Israelites into the Promised Land because of some of his mistakes.

But God used Moses to re-establish his covenant with the Israelites, and God wants to use you, too. Everything Moses did ultimately helped set up the next covenant to unfold for God's chosen people, and everything you do might set up the next stage of healing for the people you're serving. You can draw an arc from Moses's activism to Jesus's passion. As God worked through Moses, it was ultimately all leading to Christ. Can you draw an arc from your life and purpose to Jesus? Are you letting God work through you and lead people to Christ?

18
THRIVING SURVIVORS

"When the Lord saw that he had gone over to look, God called to him from within the bush, 'Moses! Moses!' And Moses said, 'Here I am.'"
~Exodus 3:4

One afternoon in the spring of 2019, the USIAHT received a call from Florida's Department of Children and Family Services. They had rescued a ten-year-old boy, let's call him Tim, who had been sold for sex by his own father since Tim was four years old. They asked us to take him into our newly-opened safe home, the only designated safe home in the country for sex-trafficked boys (as far as we know).

Tim's father was not only selling him but also his wife (Tim's mother) for over six years, up to ten times a day, likely to fuel a drug addiction or solve financial woes or both, the two most common motives for sellers.

Tim's father had threatened his wife that if she ever went to the police, he and his "partners" would kill their son. This coercion and trauma bond is not easy to break, and the cycle repeated itself for years because Tim's mother did not want her son murdered. Even more nuanced, though in her mind she was protecting him, she hesitated to celebrate Tim's birthday or send him to school or make him feel special in anyway because of the intensity of the guilt she felt for seemingly allowing him, in her mind, to be trafficked by an evil man.

When our safe home director, John, picked Tim up from a secure government housing unit in Jacksonville to take him to our safe home in Tampa, Tim brought only a trash bag filled with stuffed animals.

John looked into Tim's eyes and saw a ten-year-old boy desperate for innocence, whose childhood had been violently ripped away from him repeatedly, every day for six years, by an evil man. John also knew that most buyers of sex resembled him, a professional middle-aged white guy who was married and had kids.

As Tim got in the car, he looked up at John, holding his trash bag of stuffed animals, and asked, "Are you safe?

John was broken, "Yes, bud, I'm safe. I promise you I'm safe. And I'm taking you to a safe place where you'll be surrounded by safe people."

On the way to Tampa, John received a call from our HR director, informing him that Tim had to be taken back to Jacksonville because of a mix-up with his paperwork. His birth certificate revealed that Tim was only nine years old. Our safe home's arrangement with the state of Florida only allowed us to provide trauma-informed care for boys who were ten years old or above, one of the many stipulations in a pile of bureaucratic bull-crap we have to sift through in each case to work in lockstep with the state.

"With all due respect," John said, "I'm not taking him back. I told him he's safe; I intend to keep that promise. We'll figure this out when I get there."

Then he hung up.

"When's your birthday?" John eventually said.

Tim looked at him with innocent eyes.

"I'm ten," Tim said.

"I know you're ten," John affirmed, "but what day were you born?"

Tim looked at John cluelessly.

"Month?"

Nothing.

Tim had never celebrated his birthday, nor had any idea when it was.

When we discovered that Tim would turn ten in two weeks, John asked him one of the most dangerous questions you could ever ask a kid: "If you could have anything you want for your birthday, what would it be?"

"A balloon and a donut."

Two weeks later, our staff threw Tim his first-ever birthday party. They took him go-cart racing. They played putt-putt. They played arcade games. All they wanted to do was let Tim know he was loved, safe, special, and that he belonged. And yes, they got him a balloon and a donut.

In our trauma-informed approach, we never pushed our boys into any systematized recovery program or formulaic strategy for being reinstated into society. Kids *do* need structure, but for the first few weeks, Tim was welcome to simply get situated in his room and take the time he needed to play, rest, relax, and recover. However, we all knew the bitter reality that his recovery would take a lifetime due to the horrific things he had experienced.

Eventually, once Tim was ready, he was introduced to a trauma-informed child therapist. He told her he wanted to learn to read and go to school. He was ten years old and couldn't read a sentence.

For a year and a half, Tim went to school every day at the safe home from seven in the morning to seven at night to try to catch up to his classmates and eventually re-assimilate to a normal life. He would go on to do just that.

His mother later called us and told us they had nothing to fear anymore. Her husband had died. I'd be lying to you if I told you we didn't feel a sense of relief upon hearing this news. This person who had a hold on this woman's soul, who had a way of tracking her down wherever she was, and roping her back into being trafficked, was no more.

Tim is a hero of mine. When people applaud me for the life I made for myself as I overcame hurdles and challenges, I point instead to Tim. I point to the boys I've seen come through our safe home who, against all odds, have risen from modern-day slavery and become thriving survivors.

I think of Tim, Mary, and Billy. I think of Oree and Savanna.

Justice and Beauty
Prevention. Intervention. Rescue. Restoration.

This book intentionally does not get into the Israelites' escape from Egypt, rescue in the wilderness, journey to the Promised Land, and restoration.

Finishing the fight is up to you.

In between each of Moses's decrees to Pharaoh to let the Israelites go, Moses went back to God to consult the next move. This is its own lesson. Will you keep relying on God, remembering the burning bush and the call you received? Will you keep returning again and again in your mind to the holy ground of your purpose? Will you remember the people you stand in the gap for are not only God's people but *your* people?

The heart of God is on full display in the Exodus narrative. After four hundred and thirty years of enslavement, after warning upon warning to Pharaoh, which led to plague after plague, after extending to the Egyptians free will and grace, God proverbially said, "Enough is enough." He stepped in. All His intervening led to a rescue. He did something that only He could do. As Dr. Martin Luther King once said, "We shall overcome, because the arc of the moral universe is long, but it bends toward justice."

My friend, Stephen, who assisted me on this project, recently told me that the medieval philosopher Bonaventure defined justice with these words, "Justice makes beautiful that which had been deformed." I really, really like this notion. This goes back to the very first chapter of the Bible. In Genesis 1:27, we read "God created mankind in his own image, in the image of God he created them; male and female he created them." In our fight for justice, we must each seek to cultivate one another's God-given, sacred, holy image.

The pimps trafficking children aren't cultivating that image. Neither are the buyers of sex from children. The men in our country who are ordering children to have sex with them aren't cultivating that image, nor are they respecting themselves.

Our politicians aren't cultivating that image when they remain on the sidelines of this fight, apathetic to changing laws that would punish traffickers. Most often, politics or money obstruct politicians, government officials, and lobbyists from doing the right thing.

We must seek to make beautiful what the darkness of this world has deformed and never stop talking about the injustices darkness has caused.

Moses was a reluctant leader with insecurities about his eloquence and past, but he remained open to God's call. He had flaws and made mistakes, but learned to trust God and to lead his people. The Exodus story reminds us that God is determined to meet people where they are in their suffering and bring them through the darkness into the light. God works *in* and *through* people—like Moses, Aaron, Miriam, and countless others who joined their cause—to carry out His restoration for the world.

Jesus Christ was the ultimate rescuer and restorer. We do not worship a removed, distant, or apathetic God. Our God became a human being. He understands our deep emotions and needs because he experienced life as a man. Let's follow this same path. Let's put ourselves in the shoes of our country's children who were born in different circumstances than our own or whose lives unfolded in more traumatic ways. Let's dare to feel the deep loneliness and abandonment they must feel, just as Jesus felt every human emotion we experience. Let's fight for them, just as Jesus fought for our souls on Calvary. Let's scout the darkness of the enemy, just as Jesus defeated the powers of hell on that fateful day. Let's venture alongside these children deeper into the throes of their own persecution so that maybe, one day, they will be restored and be born again in a new life of joy and hope. Perhaps they, in Christ, can experience a resurrected life.

I invite you to echo Moses's famous words upon hearing the call of the burning bush and to do it again and again and again: "Here I am."

I LONG FOR YOU TO KNOW THE 'ONE' THAT CHANGED MY HEART...

ACKNOWLEDGMENTS

I am honored to thank the following people who played an important part in this project and many who significantly impacted my life.

First and foremost, I'd like to thank my wife, Marilyn, for all of her support, help, and encouragement throughout our 40-plus years of marriage.

I'd like to thank my amazing mom, Charlene, and dad, Jim, for giving me birth. I'm especially grateful to my mom for molding, shaping, and encouraging me with the conviction that I could make my dreams come true.

A special thanks to my daughter, Shannon, and my son, Shawn, who have taught me what love truly is.

I'd like to thank my Uncle Chosh (Jerry Malone), who provided so much in my early years and into college. His financial support was beneficial – but more importantly, taking me to the batting cages and attending all of my baseball games was foundational.

I'd like to thank my uncle and aunt, Bill (Hunley) and Patsy Lange, for doing life with Marilyn and me in the early years of our marriage. The fun and all the meals that we shared were a wonderful blessing.

So many people influenced me positively, especially in the

world of sports. Teammates, little league, high school and college coaches, and various people that I worked with or for. I'd like to thank Joe Drake, Jerry Haupt, Jim Kazora, Dan King, Dan Leasor, Jim Zerilla, and John Boles. Also, I thank Kathy Tronzo, Cobbie Harrison, Pat Jantomaso, Ron Bishop, John Zeller, Aunt Jane and Uncle Johnny Simpson. And to the UL cafeteria lady who fed me for free for many semesters.

In my professional baseball world, I'm so grateful to Lou Snipp, Al Goldis, Larry Himes, Dan Duquette, Claude Brochu, Terry Ryan, Larry Corrigan, Mike Radcliff, Peter Chernin, Chase Carey, Bob Graziano, Tommy Lasorda, Bill Geivett, and Eddie Creech.

I thank USC Dean Jim Ellis, Dr. Alan Weintraub, Kent Hamstra, and the wonderful staff at Craig Hospital for helping me by helping Shawn.

To those who helped me after my MLB career, a special thanks to Dr. John MacArthur, Dr. Will Varner, Francis Chan, Tommy Barnett, Matthew Barnett, Jerry Heuer, Tracy Williams, and Sam Eltes. And to all the pastors who prayed for me.

To those in the fight against human trafficking, I'm grateful to Geoff Rogers, Brian Robinson, Jim Perry, Jack Martin, and Lisa Vickers.

A special thanks to Jeremy Hicks and Johnny Hicks of Paper Jacket Marketing in Tampa, Florida. They've been helping us since early in the USIAHT's journey, assisting with marketing, website design, video and content creation, and campaign development.

Thank you, Stephen Copeland, for becoming my friend as we wrote this book together.

SEE MORE ABOUT USIAHT

The United States Institute Against Human Trafficking is a nationally recognized not-for-profit organization committed to ending human trafficking in the United States. Since 2016, the work of the USIAHT has led this movement of becoming the needed hub for human trafficking efforts across the nation. With multiple satellite offices around the country, we are aggressively focused on ending this massive problem happening right here in America, by fighting the demand for purchased sex from children. Our goal is to combat the consumer demand for purchased sex in the United States by creating nationwide Trafficking Free Zones, educating the public about the issue, providing help to victims and survivors, and empowering volunteer abolitionist to take a stand in their communities. We can't end child sex trafficking by ourselves, therefore we consolidate efforts for maximum effect, and partner with other organizations in this fight. **We need your help!**

LEARN MORE

An organization and movement in Las Vegas, Nevada forged from the common efforts of several key individuals, joined together in the fight to end human trafficking. We aim to do this by significantly reducing the commercial sexual exploitation of children in southern Nevada and, ultimately, the United States.

WATCH THE ADVOCATE SERIES HERE

Advocate: Defending Hope for the Hopeless is a free faith-based Small Group Study Series designed by the **U.S. Institute Against Human Trafficking** and **Kids Not For Sale** to specifically talk about how Christians and the Church, at large, can respond to the crisis of human trafficking happening in America. The purpose of the study is to evaluate the various nuances of human trafficking with a Christ-centered perspective and to spark helpful conversation among the group that leads to practical, effective solutions and understanding.